AMRIT VARSHINI

शुकल पक्ष
कृष्ण पक्ष
श्री त्वरिता नित्या

AMRIT VARSHINI

SWAMI JAYRAMDAS

Motilal Banarsidass Publications

MOTILAL BANARSIDASS
PUBLICATIONS
4741/23, Ansari Road, Daryaganj, New Delhi - 110002 (India)
Email: *mlbd@mlbd.com* | *sales@mlbd.com* | *exports@mlbd.com*
Website: *www.mlbd.com*

Amrit Varshini
by
Swami Jayramdas

First Edition Published in 2023

Published in India by Motilal Banarsidass Publications

ISBN : 978-93-91759-32-2 (HB)

Printed and bound in India

Contents

Amrit Varshini

Ambrosial Drizzle

This concept of Ambrosial Rain is very Ancient.

Back to Vedas. Mrutyurma Amritam Gamaya.

From Death to Immortality.

The aim of all these Sadhanas is surely immortality!!

As the Self is Immortal. Shri Aurobindo believed in the descent of Supramental consciousness into the human body cells.

Making this physical body Divine. Eternal as the self...

The same idea is found in the Tantras.

The third verse of the Bhootshuddi mantra says:

> Vam param Shivamritam
> Varshaya varshaya svaha

This Vam Bij or Amrita Bij Is supposed to bring down Ambrosial Rain.

Nectar from the Paramshiva consciousness above the Sahasrar.

Abode of ShivShakti Union. An Alchemy created by transformed sexual fluid.

Ojas Soma along with endocrine secretions.

Lam Shambhava Shariram Utpadaya Utpadaya Svaha.

Bringing the creation of a new Shiva body.

A Descent of the Supreme into the Physical.

The concept of the Chiranjeevis like Dattatreya, Hanuman, Bali, Gorakhnath, and others matches with this theory of Immortality!!

The question remains.

Is it possible in this Kaliyuga to achieve this Aim through those Sadhanas? Amrita Varshini is more a question mark than a reality. Still to be gained and achieved by pure Selfless Sadhaks. Iron into Gold.

DEDICATION

I dedicate this short work at the lotus feet of my most Revered Guru Shri Dhyan Yogi Madhusudan dasji Maharaj to whom I owe my very life on the spiritual path and who inspired me to write for the benefit of Youth and English reading seekers.

All inspiring words are his; defects are my own!

"O, Lord! By which path can the embodied soul become one with the supreme reality? Have compassion on me, O Lord! I bow to your feet.

The Devi (Guru Gita)

PREFACE

Although Kundalini Yoga belongs to the Tantric school, the turn it receives from the great Siddha Gurus goes totally beyond Human concepts, interpretations, scriptures, and rites!

Spirituality is not to be found in books and learned discourses; it remains the concealed property of the enlightened Ones, who, from time immemorial, HAVE maintained the power of tradition alive.

Divine is their Abode, Divine are their realization, immersed in streams of Bliss, they embody Divine Grace on Earth!

Their company and blessings are the only true features of Yoga. Kundalini Awakening without Shaktipat is a dangerous endeavour. Practices deprived of guidance are bound to fail.

The Great Goddess who creates, maintains, and destroys this Universe is the primary cause of individual spiritual evolution. This Divine Power, Coiled, can only answer to the call of Divine Men and uplifting aspirations. She is hard of access and known alone to the pure-hearted selfless Yogis. Her rising from slumber puts an end to Ignorance, bondage, and disharmony. She is pure bliss, Knowledge, and consciousness, beyond, dualities and spiritual injunctions, the very source of true Love, Beauty, nectar Divine.

The Living Grace of Shri Guru, the destroyer of Darkness, the life force purifier annihilates the mind and enlightens the Intellect.

Her multi-faced triple aspect challenges, all adorations, and baffles all descriptions!

We have just tried in this book to achieve a synthesis of the main features of the practice of Kundalini Yoga. Of course, they cannot replace the direct touch and live power of a Master. They just aim at drawing guide lines for the intelligent seeker among the intricacies and vastness of spiritual life.

We just hope and pray they will serve their purpose.

April 14th, 96

-Jay Ramdas

FOREWORD

Shri Jayramdas has been a very devoted and very inquisitive disciple of Revered Dhyanayogi Shri Madhusudandasji Maharaj for the last few decades and isa brotherly co-disciple of mine devoted as we are to this great Dhyana-yogi, he is known to me since more than a couple of decades.

The Amritvarshini, authored by Jayramdas, is a comprehensive monograph discussing the body and detailing all useful information that a sincere disciple of Shri Dhyanayogiji Maharaj needs to know at some point or other during his progress on the path of Sadhana. Shri Jayramdas has taken great interest in our ancient scriptures and relevant Tantric literature in collating all aspects of the Rajayoga to which Shri Dhyanayogiji introduced his disciple by the process of Shaktipat, and consequently awakening his Kundalini, which fact manifested as various symptoms like Pranotthana, different Kriyas like Pranayama, Asanas, Mudras, etc. in the physical bodies of the Sadhakas during their Dhyana sessions every day.

He has succeeded in achieving a synthesis of the main features of Kundalini yoga, which will surely serve to guide the aspirant in grasping this process intellectually and make him conversant with the intricacies and greatness of spiritual life. Shri Jayramdas deserves our congratulations for accomplishing this useful aid on the path of Shre Gurudev Dhyanayogiji.

Dr Narayan Kansara
Director (retd)
Maharshi Academy of Vedic Science, Ahmedabad
16th August 1996

ॐ

श्री स्वामी जगद्गुरु शंकराचार्य पीठ करवीर

२२९९, डी वार्ड, शुक्रवार पेठ, कोल्हापूर

५-६-९६

WE ARE VERY GLAD TO GO THROUGH A PRECIOUS BOOK NAMED " अमृत वर्षिणी " (AMRUT VARSHEENNEE) WRITTEN BY SHREE JAY- RAMADASA, WHO HAD BEEN INSPIRED AND GUIDED BY HIS GURU, HIS HOLINESS SHREE DHYAN YOGEE MADHUSUDAN DASJEE MAHARAJ -(ध्यानयोगी श्री मधुसूदनदासजी महाराज)- WITH SO MANY BLESSINGS AND SURELY FOLLOWED THE PRECEPTS OF THE GURU-PARAMPARA.

MAY THIS WORK BE OF IMMENSE HELP TO SEEKERS OF YOGA. THESE ARE OUR'S CHOICEST BLESSINGS.

HIS HOLINESS(1008 SWAMI SHREE VIDYASHANKAR BHARTI)

विद्याशंकर भारती स्वामी.

J. SHAKRACHARYA KARVIRPITH

KOLHAPUR.

PART 1

THE NADIS AND THE FIVE VITAL AIRS

THE NADIS

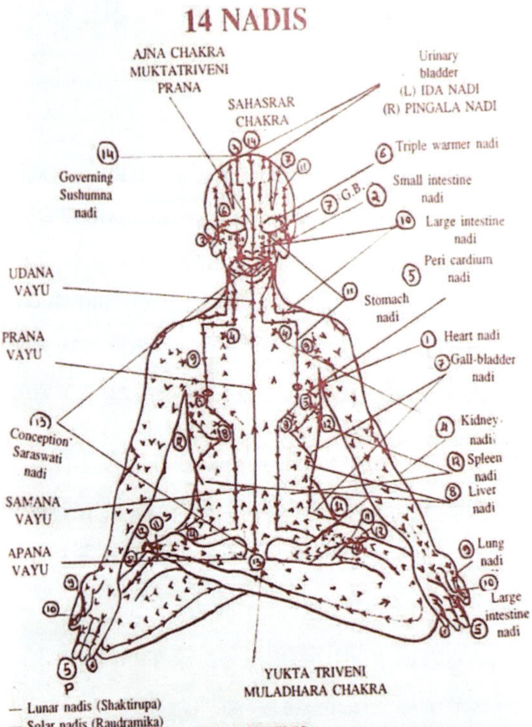

ENERGY'S FLOW

(1) Heart [L] (Armpit to Small Finger) (2) Small intestine [S] (Small Finger to Ear) (3) Urinary Bladder [S] (From upper nose to small toe) (4) Kidneys [L] (From sole to shoulder) (5) Pericardium (From heart to majorf) (6) Triple warmer [S] (Ringf to Eye brow) (7) Gall-bladder [S] (outer eye to 4th toe) (8) Liver [L] (Big toe to rib) (9) Lungs [L] (Shoulder to thumb) (10) Large intestine [S] (index to nostril) (11) Stomach [S] (Left eye to 2nd toe) (12) Spleen [L] (Big toe to rib)

The scriptures reveal that the physical body which is a product of Food possesses 8 components. Hair, blood, flesh, and fat are said to come from the mother; while bone, muscle, marrow, and semen come from the father.

This physical body is composed of 2/3 of Water along with gelatin, fat, lime phosphate, albumin, and fibrin. These substances contain hydrogen, carbon, nitrogen, calcium, and phosphorus. As such this physical frame would be an only lifeless matter if it was not permeated by this very subtle life force known as PRANA. Prana, the cosmic vital force has a five-fold action on the physical body which keeps a constant balance between the three humors, Wind (VAT), Bile (PIT), and Phlegm (KAF).

The five vital airs PRANA, APANA, UDANA, SAMANA, and VYANA control different functions of the physical body. The flow of their energy moves through subtle channels or ducts called in Sanskrit "NADIS" from the root Nad' (movement). These Nadis are not the nerves of the nervous system, nor veins or arteries. They are the subtle lines of energy allowing all vital functions in the body. These Nadis are enumerable in number; certain Tantras speak of 72000, others of 300000, they are variously described in the Yoga Upanishads, Tantras, and Ayurvedic treatises. Out of these 14 are the most important. They are known as Yoga Nadis: Sushumna, Saraswati, Ida, Pingala, Pusa, Varuna, Hastijihva, Yasaswini, Alambusa, Kuhu, Gandhari, Shankhini, Payasvini and Visvodara. In the Yogic treatises out of those 14 Nadis, only 4 achieve prominent action and position: the Sushumna, the Saraswati, the Ida, and the Pingala.

The Sushumna is the chief of all those Nadis, it flows through the spinal cord and becomes active when the Kundalini is awakened. The Saraswati is the counterpart of the Sushumna. Both these Nadis form an independent energy circulation, distinct from the twelve others, which are at work in everyone. They hold high spiritual functions and have a direct connection with the organs and can strengthen, purify the main energetic system.

The Ida and Pingala run on the sides of the spine and carry the subtle energy of the sympathetic chains of the autonomous system. Ida is a lunar duct while Pingala is solar. Both are the chief of the 12 Nadis divided into 6 Lunar or negative ducts and 6 solar or positive ducts. The solar or positive Nadis are so-called as they are situated on the outer side of a limb and answer to organs that are in contact with the outer world. Those are the workshop organs thattransform outer elements into energy and blood. (Stomach, two intestines, gall bladders, urinary bladder, triple-warmer), in fact, functions that produce heat (respiratory, digestive, and genitor urinary.) These ducts are also exposed to the sun which generates a vital force (Prana) and activates the system.

The Lunar or negative Nadis are situated on the inner part of the limbs, they answer to organs that purify the blood and make it circulate (heart, lungs, spleen, pancreas, liver, kidneys, and pericardium). Their energy works in-depth, while solar ones are more on the surface. The moon cools down and is related to the mind; it brings soothing rays and nectar; it allows peace, and rest while the sun is related to Prana or activity, life in general. For keeping the body sound and healthy, a regulated breath is essential alternately through the two nostrils: during daytime through the left or lunar nostril, which gives health and prolongs life, and at night through the right solar nostril.

Food taken when energy flows through the right nostril helps digestion. When the left one is more active it worsens digestion. When both nostrils breathe equally simultaneously, it means that the vital force flows through the central duct in the spine, it is the time best suited for concentration and meditation.

The normal flow of the vital force in the 12 Nadis starts from:

1. The Heart duct going from the armpit to the small finger is lunar, negative.
2. Small intestine duct, small finger to ear, temple; it is solar, positive.
3. Urinary bladder, upper nose to the small toe, it is solar, positive.
4. Kidneys

Thus, the energy flows alternately in two lunar ducts, then in two solar ones. The highest intensity of energy flow in one duct lasts for about two hours: Out of the solar ducts, 3 carry the energy from the fingers to the head and 3 from the head to the toes. While of the lunar ducts 3 carry the energy from the chest to the fingers and 3 from the toes to the chest.

These different ducts have different actions or reactions to each other. On the course of each of these ducts are found several sensitive spots which when used in the right manner are supposed to cure different diseases. The flow of energy is used to tone up the organ ahead and to quiet down the following one, or to quiet down by slowing down the organ ahead and toning up the following organ.

However, this normal flow of energy can be easily changed and modified by advanced Yogis. The energy starts from the lung duct at dawn.

(1) The Lung duct: Its pulse is between the right wrist and the apophyse in depth. It flows from3 a.m. to 5 a.m., it is lunar or negative. The sensitive points on its course cure diseases of the lungs, trachea, pharynx, and larynx. It starts in the space between the shoulder, the upper part of the left chest goes down the inner part of the shoulder, the arm and passes through the middle of the inner part of the arm, and ends at the inner part of the thumb.

(2) The Large intestine Duct: Its pulse is in between the apophyse and the right wrist on the surface. It flows from 5 a.m. to 7 a.m., it is solar and positive. Its sensitive points cure diseases of the head, including the face, eye, ear nose, and throat.

It starts from the outer part of the left index goes up to the hand up the wrist, moves up the arm in the middle up to the elbow level, then making a curve it goes up to the top of the shoulder, makes a curve backward and comes back in the front and lower part of the neck goes up the neck crosses the lower and upper maxilla just in front of the left nostril and ends on the left side of the left nostril.

(3) The Stomach duct: Its pulse is at the apophyse level of the right hand on the surface. It flows from 7 a.m. to 9 a.m., it is solar and positive. Its sensitive points cure diseases- of the head, face, chest, abdomen; gastro-intestinal tract.

It starts under the left eye in the middle, goes down between the nose and cheek, down to the left side of the mouth, then goes down the lower 'maxilla makes a right angle, crosses the upper maxilla passes in between the ear and the cheek, crosses the temple and stops at the root of the hair, then starts going down the neck making a right angle near the collar bone and goes down the chest bp to the middle of the breast, slightly curves and goes down near the abdominal muscles down to the lower end in the pubic region, then slightly curves and goes down the upper part of the thigh up to the knee goes down the shin-bone, crosses the left outer part of the foot' and ends on the second toe near the nail.

(4) The Spleen duct: Its pulse is at the level of the apophyse right hand, depth. It flows from 9 a.m. to 11 a.m., it is lunar and negative. Its sensitive points are used to cure diseases of the gastro intestinal tract and Genito urinary system.

It starts from the big toe near the nail goes up the foot, passes in the inner side of the leg near the shin bone, then near the knee goes up the inner part of the thigh up to the upper part of the pubis, crossing the thigh in the middle, it takes a straight line up to the lower end of the ribs up to the point where the left arm joins the chest, then it makes a slight curve and ends in the inner part of the ribs, 3rd or 4th.

(5) The Heart duct: Its pulse is in between the left wrist and the apophyse in depth. It flows from 11 a.m. up to 1 p.m., It is lunar and negative. Its sensitive, points are used to cure diseases of the heart and mental disorders.

It starts from the space where the chest and the arm meet, then moves through the inner part of the arm inner part of the elbow up to the inner part of the wrist, and goes through the inner part of the hand (palm) and ends at the small finger.

(6) The Small Intestine duct: Its pulse is in between the apophyse and the left wrist on the surface. It flows from 1 p.m. up to 3p.m., It is solar, positive. Its points are used to cure diseases of the occipital region, eye, and ear shoulder.

It starts from the outer part of the small finger near the nail, goes up the outer part of the hand up to the wrist, then behind the elbow, and moves in a straight line just behind the shoulder making an angle that goes up to the middle of the shoulder blade, making a curve again moves upward to the lower and back part of the neck, it moves on the left side and middle of the neck, with a slight curve, crosses the maxilla up to the cheek with a slight curve again and ends at the outer part of the ear, down the temple.

(7) The Urinary Bladder duct: Its pulse is after the apophyse of the left wrist on the surface. It flows from 3p.m. up to 5p.m., It is solar and positive. The sensitive points cure diseases of the head, neck, back, lumbar region, and anus.

It starts in the space between the upper part of the nose and eye, crosses the forehead up to the cranium, moves around the cranium goes down the back part of the neck in the middle, goes down the back on the left side of the spine down to the upper part of the buttock then making an angle, goes upwards a little near the spine and goes down again near the point the two buttocks joint, then goes down the left buttock in the middle, goes down the thigh on its backside down to the point behind the knee, after making a right angle on the left, it moves upwards again through the thigh and the outer part of the buttock; the next point starts at the upper part of the shoulder blade; it makes a straight line on the left of the first one, which was closer to the spine, its last point is on the top of the buttock. The next point starts behind the knee and goes down the calf muscle; after a slight curve, it goes down the outer part of the heel and then moves on the outer part of the foot down to the small toe.

(8) The Kidney duct: Its pulse is after the apophyse of the left wrist in depth. It flows from 5p.m. up to 7p.m. It is lunar and negative. The points are used to cure diseases of the genital urinary system.

It starts in the middle under the sole of the left foot and then moves upward on the inner part of the foot, making a kind of circle a little up the heel moves upward passes near the calf muscle, and continues upwards on the inner part of the thigh up to the pubic region. It goes upward on the line of the abdominal muscles parallel to the Saraswati duct up to the lower end of the last abdominal muscle, then makes a slight curve towards the chest and follows a straight line parallel to the sternum bone, crossing the breast it ends just before the shoulder level.

(9) The Pericardium duct: Its pulse is after the apophyse of the right wrist in depth. It flows from 7 p.m. to 9 p.m.; it is lunar and negative. Its points are used to cure diseases of the heart, pericardium, and mental disorders.

It starts from the heart, moves upward to the lower level of the shoulder then goes down the arm following the course of the humerus bone in a strayline on the inner part of the arm, then reaches the inner part of the wrist crosses the palm following the inner part of the major finger up to the nail.

(10) The Triple Warmer duct: Its pulse is after the apophyse of the right wrist on the surface)It flows from 9 p.m. to 11 p.m., it is solar and positive. Its points are used to cure diseases of the lateral aspect of the head, ear, and hypochondrium.

It starts near the nail of the ring finger moves upward on the outer part of the finger, crosses the hand up to the wrist, moves upward on the outer part of the arm passes near the elbow on the right, and continues to go upward the arm reaching the back part of the shoulder making a curve it moves upward parallel to the collar bone up to the lower part of the neck at the back moves up the neck its outer part to reach the lower part of the ear, then goes around the ear (outer) up to its upper root and through a line it reaches the outer part of the eyebrow.

(11) The Gall bladder duct: Its pulse is at the level of the apophyse of the left wrist on the surface. It flows from 11p.m. to 1 a.m.; it is solar and positive. Its points are used to cure diseases of the lateral aspect of the head, hypochondrium, and liver gall bladder.

It starts from the outer part of the eye, following a line it crosses the cheek up to the middle of the ear root, it makes a curve and moves upwards crossing the temple it stops in the hair at the level of the forehead on, the side of the head, making a sharp angle it goes down again to the level of the temple describes a semi-circle around the outer ear up to the lower part of the cranium again making a sharp angle it describes a semi-circle on the side of the cranium up to the forehead where it makes again a sharp angle and goes around the cranium, nearly parallel to the urinary bladder duct down to the lower end of the cranium at the back. It goes down the neck following the line of the muscles, then makes a curve, crosses the collar bone in the middle, passing near the shoulder it continues and passes near the lower and inner part of the armpit, then it makes an angle up to the third rib, making again an angle it reaches the side of the body near the hip. Making an angle it goes down the upper part of the pubis. Making an angle it crosses the upper part of the thigh and reaches the middle and side of the buttock, then it goes down the side of the outer part of the thigh up to the level of the knee, follows the outer part of the calf muscle, crosses the ankle and the upper part of the foot to reach the fourth toe near the nail.

(12) The Liver duct: Its pulse is at the level of the apophyse of the left wrist in depth. It flows from 1 a.m. to 3 a.m. It is lunar and negative. Its points are used to cure diseases of the liver and Genito urinary system.

It starts on the left side of the nail of the big toe, goes up the foot up to the ankle, makes a curve to move upward on the inner part of the tibia, follows the inner part of the calf muscle, and passes near the knee, goes up the inner part of the thigh up to the public region, moves upward to the hip and ends near the fifth rib.

It joins the Lung duct at the heart plexus. All these ducts or Nadis are presided by different deities: Shiva is the deity of the central duct Sushumna.

Hari is the deity of the Ida Nadi (left nostril)

Brahma is the deity of the Pingala Nadi (right nostril) Viraj is the deity of the Saraswati Nadi (counterpart of the Sushumna)

Pusan is the deity of the Pusa Nadi.

Vayu is the deity of the Varuna Nadi.

Varuna is the deity of the Hastijihva.

The Lord of hunger is the deity of the Kuhu Nadi.

Fourth Avarana, the Catur - Dasara Chakra

The 4th Avarana has, for this Prakriti, the mahamaya Bija ईं (इम् Im) which is kamakala, it suggests Paramesvar associated with Maya, the cause of all the universe, a mind devoted to Isvara Vicara and the modification of such a mind this chakra is called Sarva-saubhagya-dayaka, the bestower of all bliss. Paramesvar bestowsthe knowledge of undifferentiated oneness, exterminating all differences and miseries caused by the Triputi.

The Sampradaya yoginis of the Chakra are prominently given.

The Jagad guru is the embodiment of traditional knowledge. He is the cause of this universe as well as the liberator of it. He pervades the macrocosm of the fourteen worlds. This Avarana represents these worlds in each of its fourteen triangles, which suggest one inquiry about Paramesvar. The fourteen Avarana Devatas of this Chakra are the modifications of the mind that have taken the form of the above Paramesvaras.

1 Akasadhi – karana, Akasa

2 Pranadhi – Karana, Vayu

3 Jyotirdarsan – Karana, Tejas

4 Anand – Maya – Karana, Rasa

5 Indra Pranadhi – Karana,Prajnana, Pratardana, Mukhya Prana

6 Vaisvanaradhi – Karana, having the three worlds as body

7 Dyubh - Vadyadhi – Karana, the earth, interspace, and heaven

8 Sarvatra - Prasiddhya – Karana,being all mind, superimposed by ignorance (Avidya)

9 Attradhi – Karana , Sarvasamharaka

10 Guhadhi – Karana , Paharakasa

11 Antaradhi – Karana, Possessed of Dharmas

12 Antarya - myadhi – Karana , controller of the world

13 Adrsyat - vadhi – Karana , Adrsya , Anirdrsya

14 Bhumadhi – Karana, all pervading one without a second

Tripuravasini is the Cakreswari of the enclosure.The triad Pramatr, Prameya and Pramana is known by the name of Triputi. Tripuravasini means the destroyer of misery caused bythis Triputi (the triad knower, knowable, and knowledge). Ishitva Siddhi and sarvavasankari Mudra are worshipped in this Chakra.

The Chakra is in the form of a complex figure having fourteen triangles, each of these triangles being inscribed with the fourteen consonants beginning with "Ka" and finishing with "Dha". These triangles symbolize also the powers of the Goddess, which are thought of as presiding over the fourteen main subtle ducts in the human body (Nadis).

Meditation on Isvara:

1 Sarva - samksobini, the power to make everything restless. It corresponds to the Alambusa Nadi (the Limit) starting from the central channeland reaching the anus and to the letter Ka. It is linked to Apana Vayu and MuladharaChakra.

2 Sarva - Vidravini, the power to disperse. It corresponds to the Kuhu Nadi (the hidden, the new moon), starting from both the sides of the central channel and reachingthe penis, and to the letter Kha. It is linked to Apana Vayu and svadhisthan Chakra.

3 Sarva - Karsini, the power to attract all, is associated with the Visvodhara Nadi (the carrier of all), located inside and all around the stomach and the navel and with the letter Ga. It is linked to Samana Vayu.

4 Sarva - Hladini, the power of conferring delight. It is associated with the Varana (or Varuna) Nadi (the pervader),

extending upwards and downwardsfrom the same region and with the letter Gha.

5 Sarva – (Sam) Mohini, the power of confusing, corresponding toHasti – Jihva Nadi (the Elephant Tounge), beginning at the right side of Ida and going to the left toe, and the letter Na.

6 Sarve – Stambhini, the power to sustain, corresponding to the Yasovati Nadi, (Abounding in Glory), and to the letter Ca.

7 Sarva – Jrmbhini, the power to expand, is associated with Payasvini Nadi, (Full of Juice), and with the letter Cha.

8 sarva – Vasamkari, the power of influence, associated with Gandhari Nadi (musical note E) and the letter Ja.

9 Sarva - Ranjani, the power to please, corresponding to the Pusa Nadi (the Nourisher) and the letter Jha.

10 Sarvan – Madini, the power to intoxicate, corresponding to the Samkhini Nadi (the Sea Shell) and the letter Na.

11 Sarvartha – Sadhani, the power to accomplish all aims, associated withSaraswati Nadi (the Goddess) and with the letter Ta.

12 Sarva – Sampatti – Purani, the power to fulfill, corresponding to the Ida Nadi (the Inspirer) and the letter Tha. It is linked to the third eye.

13 Sarva – mantramayi, the power consisting of all mantras, corresponding to the Pingala Nadi 9 the Red) and to the letter Da, again linked to the third eye. Finally

14 Sarva – Dvanda – Ksayamkari, the power to destroy duality, associated with Sushumna Nadi, (the Gracious, the Blissful)

and with the letter Dha and linked to the spine.

One commentary of Bhaskara–Raya goes thus:

" the fourteen Nadis are the fourteen powers of Sri Chakra. So, the Sri Yantra not only represents the mind with all its Vrittis and different levels of consciousness but also the body with all its Pranas and ten digestive fires and now the flow of Prana strengthen by Bij Mantras in the fourteen Yoga Nadis or ducts of vital energy. "

Definite therapies can be used with the help of these Matrka Mantras in these Chakra and Nadi systems. Bija mantraacupuncture as Research Work.

The Moon (Chandra) is the deity of the Gandhari and Shankhini Nadis. Prajapati is the deity of the Payasvini Nadi. Lord Pavaka is the deity of the Visvodara Nadi.

The vital energy which flows in the different ducts is divided into 5 main currents and 5 subsidiary ones: 5 Pranas (Prana, Apana, Udana, Samaná, Vyana) and 5 Upa-pranas: (Naga, Kurma, Krikara, Devadatta, Dhananjaya)

Each of these vital airs has different functions, locations, and colors.

(1) The **Prana** has its seat in the respiratory system, lungs, heart, and medulla oblongata, it moves in the mouth, the nostrils, the throat, the navel, and the big toes of the feet above and below the Kundalini. Its deity is Visishta. Its functions are breathing, inhaling, exhaling, and coughing. It is of yellow and sapphire color.

(2) The **Apana** has its seat in the anus region, it moves in the genitals thighs, knees, belly, hip shanks, navel, and the hole of the rectal fire.: Its deity is Visvasrishta. This vital air has a downward course, working the evacuation of faces, urine, and semen. Its color is orange-red or an evening cloud color.

(3) The **Samana** has its seat in the region of the navel. It pervades the hands and feet and all parts of the body. It spreads the partaken food converted into blood. Its deity is Jaya. It works to nourish the body and kindles the bodily fire of the digestive system. Its color is green or milky.

(4) The **Udana** has its seat in the region of the throat. It moves in all the joints. Its deity is Aja. Its function is accelerative and disruptive. It works through afferent fibres. It has an upward course, it keeps a person standing erect on its legs. It works deglutition. During sleep, it separates the astral body from the physical one. At the time of death, it takes the incarnated soul to God. It flows through the Sushumna Nadi when the Kundalini awakens. Its color is violet blue (the color of fire).

(5) The **Vyana:** has its location in the Sahasar chakra; it moves in the ears, eyes, hip, ankles, heels, nose, neck, and buttocks. Its deity is Vishvayoni.

(6) Construction and upbuilding are is functions: it work during giving up and seizing. Its color is rose and silver. The functions of the five subsidiary vital airs are as follows:

 (1) Naga helps with belching and vomiting.

 (2) Kurma helps the opening and closing of the eyelids.

(3) Krikara produces hiccups and helps with sneezing.

(4) Devadatta produces yawns.

(5) Dhananjaya produces phlegm and helps the swelling of the body. These are however included in the five main currents.

These five vital airs keep a constant balance between the three humours of the body.

From the toe to the navel is the seat of wind (VAAT). From the navel to the throat is the seat of fire (PITT).

From the throat to the head is the seat of water, phlegm (KAF).

If any of the three become out of balance, illness results.

This imbalance can be however corrected using herbs, the practice of asanas, pranayama, and the awakening of Kundalini.

What matters for yogis is to control the vital force (prana) and make it flow in the central duct of the spine. Therefore, awaken the Kundalini.

The Lunar Ida Nadi and the solar Pingala Nadi carry out only the ordinary functions of the body, while the Sushumna and Saraswati Nadis hold a higher spiritual role.

The Sushumna or central duct starts from the second vertebra of the coccygeal region, flows through the spinal cord up to the top of the head, and ends at the upper lip.

Usually, the Sushumna refers to the gross spinal cord and is divided into three subtle layers: The Vajra Nadi of fire, the Chitra Nadi, and the Brahma Nadi.

The Sushumna has the grossest form and is tamasic (inertia).

Its color is red. Within the Sushumna, we find the Vajra Nadi, which is solar and contains rajasic qualities (activity).

Within this Vajra Nadi, we find the Chitra Nadi, which is of sattvic (purity) nature, lunar, and pale color.

And finally, within the Chitra Nadi,we find a very minute canal, the Brahma Nadi(canalis centralis) through which the Kundalini rises once awakened.

The lower end of the Chitra Nadi through which the Kundalini will enter is called Brahmadwara (Door of Brahma) by Yogis; this Nadiis like the thin thread of a lotus stalk, brilliant, shining with five colors, it is also known as the heavenly way, the royal path leading to liberation.

These three Nadis in one constitute the triple aspect of the Godhead. The Sushumna acts on physical strength as well as moral and mental (brain and spinal cord.) The sensitive points on its course are used for diseases of the head, neck, back, and lumbar region.

The Saraswati Nadi which has a direct connection with the Sushumna is like its counterpart on the other side of the body. It starts above the sex organ passes through the middle of the body up to the lower lip and ends at the base of the tongue. It acts on three systems: breathing, digestive, and Genito urinary.

Its sensitive spots help the cure of diseases of the chest, abdomen, pharynx, and Larynx. In the Kundalini Upanishad, it is said: "The Kundalini is awakened only by the rousing of the Saraswati". Merely by shaking the Saraswati one is cured of dropsy, jalodara, gulma (diseases of the stomach), pliha (spleen disease).

The Saraswati Nadi is said to have sound in her womb and

should be shaken daily, this Nadi is also called Arundhati which literally means : "Helping the performance of good actions".

"Earth, Water, Fire, Air, Ether, consciousness, intellect and ego: thus my Prakriti has been divided into eight parts (Bg. Gita 7.4)"

Up till now we have described the course of the different Nadis in the body, the work of the five vital airs (Prana), the role they play on the functioning of the physical body. This Physical body is the Sheath of food (annamaya kosha) where the three elements, earth, water, fire are reigning.

The 14 Nadis, the 5 Pranas, the 5 Upa-pranas, and the five (Karmaindriyas) organs of action constitute the vital sheath, (pranamaya kosha) It's presiding elements are Air and Ether. Those two sheaths allow all immediate functions of the physical body perceived by all. But man possesses still more subtle sheaths which go beyond the reach of the human eye. They are the seats of mind and consciousness.

The Mental sheath (manomaya kosha) is a combination of the mind (manas) and the five senses of knowledge (Jnanaindriyas) and the Vijnanamaya kosha which is formed by the same senses of knowledge but associated with the intellect (buddhi). The last sheath is known as the sheath of bliss (anandamaya kosha).

The physical body or gross body is called Sthula sharira.

The vital sheath, the mental and knowledge sheaths constitute the subtle body (sukshma sarira or linga sarira), the inner instrument (antakarana). This subtle body contains in itself the cause of rebirth into the gross body.

The sheath of bliss represents the Causal body (Karan sharira). It is so called because it holds the potentiality of making stored past life impressions to fructify and weave around it a fresh body, able to develop and evolve with the mental and intellectual capacities gained during a previous birth. The seat of the Self is known as the Maha Karan sharira. When the soul enters the body of the baby after the sixth month in the womb, its consciousness penetrates through the head and goes down the spine.

Thus the spinal cord is the duct adored by the yogis with the Kundalini at its root near the coccyx, in the plexus called Mooladhar. The spinal column is referred to in yogic treatises as the Meru Danda or axis of the body like Mount Meru is the Axis of the earth.

The spine is formed by a series of 33 bones, the vertebraedivided into (5 regions)

1) Coccygeal region (imperfect vertebrae coccyx, 4 verte brae)
2) Sacral region (sacrum, buttocks level, 5 vertebrae)
3) Lumbar region (waist, 5 vertebrae)
4) Dorsal region (back 12 vertebrae)
5) Cervical region (neck *7* vertebrae)

The five regions of the spine correspond to the seat of the 5 Chakras, (Muladharaa, Svadhishthan Manipura, Anahata, and Vishudha) which are found on the grey portion of the spinal cord. This spinal cord is a column of soft grey and white matter. White matter surrounds grey matter which in its turn surrounds the canalis centralis. This canal in the middle is the seat of the subtle Brahma Nadi, running from the Mooladhar (root plexus) to the Sahasrar (top of the head). It is through this duct that the awakened Kundalini proceeds upward.

The grey matter layer is the seat of the subtle Chitra Nadi while the white matter one is the seat of the Vajra Nadi. The Sushumna Nadi is often used to refer to the whole of the spinal cord. The Chakras (plexuses) or Padmas (Lotuses) are in the ethereal body, they cannot be seen by ordinary physical eyes but can be felt, visualized, and experienced during spiritual practices. They have corresponding centres in the spinal cord and control the function of particular centres of the gross body. They are how we maintain contact with the physical world, the vital world, the mental world, and still higher spheres. They represent the different planets and spheres of the mini-universe at work within man.

According to Shri Aurobindo

1) The Muladharaa rules the physical up to the subconscious.
2) The Svadhisthan rules the lower vital being.
3) The Manipura rules the higher vital being.
4) The Anahata rules the emotional and psychic being.
5) The Vishudha rules mental expression.
6) The Ajna rules the dynamic mental, the process of the will.
7) The Sahasrar Rules the higher thinking mental, process of intuition, the illumined mental process, and higher states.

These Lotuses represent the subtle aspects of spiritual

evolution. Although the Lotus is known to grow in mud it remains immune and pure among watery and muddy surroundings, like the chakras which continue their action among the impurities and fluidity of the world.

The petals of the chakras are figures formed by the position of the Nadis on that particular centre and by the different rays received from the different worlds.: The vibration produced at each petal is represented by a corresponding Sanskrit letter. When the Kundalini is asleep the petals lie downward, when she awakes, they turn upwards. At each chakra, a particular element (tattva) preponderates which is denoted by a special color, the seed letter of that element, the vital air working at this level, and a presiding deity with its Shakti and Shaktis presiding over (physical components).

A certain animal denotes that the plexus has the qualities of that animal and that the motion of the Kundalini resembles its motion at this level. This animal is also the vehicle of the Element corresponding. In each petal are found special Vrittis (mental modifications) denoting aspects of the level of consciousness at this chakra. Certain symbols describe the corresponding element, denoting the different levels of consciousness with their corresponding worlds and spheres.

The whole Chakra system is associated with the Hamsa Vidya, the natural soul moves through the evolution of Prana and consciousness.

(2) THE DESCRIPTION OF THE CHAKRAS IN SAUNDARYA LAHARI OF SHRI SHANKARACHARYA

"In the thousand-petalled lotus, Sahasrar,
You sport with your Lord in secret,
Having traversed the entire path of Kundalini,
The element earth in Mooladhar, water in Svadhisthana,
Fire in Manipura, Air in Anahata, Ether in Vishuddhi
And the mind in Ajna between the eye-brows." *V*. 9.

"Oh! Glorious One, drenching all the veins with
The nectar dripping from your feet, from the
Dizzy heights you descend to your abode and
Turning yourself into a serpentine coil, sleep
In the fine hole of the Lotus root, Mooladhar." V. 10.

This poetry of Adi Shankaracharyahas been associated with some Tantrik Prayogas and the same vidya is called Shadakskari Vidya to achieve worldly purposes. It seems that these prayogas were added later on by some Tantriks. Difficult to verify its origins.

"I venerate the supreme creator of bliss
Abiding in your Ajna chakra between the eyebrows
Resplendent like millions of suns and moons,
Adorned on his side by the supreme power,
Meditating on whom with devotion, one lives

In the effulgent world which needs no light
And is beyond the reach of the sun, moon, and fire." V. 36.

"I worship the Auspicious One residing in your
Vishuddhi chakra, shining like a pure crystal
The creator of ether and you the Goddess of
Identical disposition; by their radiance
Resembling moonlight, the World enveloped in
The darkness of Ignorance rejoices like the chakori
Birds bathing in the rays of the Moon." V. *37.*

"I worship the two unique swans Ham and Sah
Floating in the minds of the great, whoever
Enjoy the honey in the full-blown lotus of
Knowledge and from whose prattle shine the eighteen
Arts and who sift Good from Evil, like milk from water." V. 38.

"I worship the blue cloud hued One, who has
Sought refuge in your Manipura chakra
Adorned with the effulgent lightning
Destroyer of Darkness; shines with the bow of Indra,
Studded with various lustrous gems and rains
Mercy on the three worlds burnt by the Destroyer
In the great dissolution." V. 40.

"Oh, Mother! I bow to the Destroyer whoever remains
In your Svadhisthan Chakra, taking the form of Fire,

And to the Great Power, whose glance, tender, wet with Kindness protects by cool healing when the angry Look of the Destroyer burns the worlds during the Great dissolution." V. 39.

"I meditate on the Nine-faceted One, dancing the Great cosmic dance with the nine moods and the Dance loving power in your Mooladhar." V. 41.

(3) THE CHAKRAS

(1) THE MULADHARAA CHAKRA

(Illustration by Swami Jayramdas)

The Muladhara chakra is located at the base of the spinal cord; it lies between the origin of the reproductory organ and the anus. Two fingers above the anus and about two fingers below the genitals, this space is four fingers in width. It is just below the Kand and the junction where the Ida, Pingala, and Sushumna Nadis meet (Yukta Triveni).

Mula means root and Adhara support; it is the root of the Sushumna and the support of the six chakras. It is also referred to as Bhuta Sringat or junction, Knot of Merging, and Mula Sringat (root junction). It is also called Sumeru which represents the Axis of the Universe. The color of this chakra is crimson, it has four petals from which four important Nadis emanate.

The subtle vibrations produced by these Nadis are represented by the Sanskrit letters (Vam Sham Sham Sam)

VAM represents pure water, Brahma, Rajas Guna, and the Bij of the R̲igveda.

SHAM represents White, the giver of virtues. Wealth and the fulfiller of desires, Vishnu, Sattva Guna, and the Bij of the Yajurveda.

SHHAM represents the pure, giver of all fruits, Rudra, Tamo guna, and the bij of the Samaveda.

SAM is the cause of All, the Shakti, the Bij of the Atharvaveda.

These four Bij mantras vibrate in the Sushumna, the four petals contain the Vrittis (modifications) of the four forms of Beatitude: Paramananda (supreme bliss), Sahajananda (natural bliss), Yogananda (Yogic bliss), and Viraanda (Heroic bliss).

These four petals represent the four Ages (Satya Yuga, Treta Yuga, Dvapara Yuga, and Kali Yuga)

The four oceans of sugar cane, wine, ghee, and milk.

Each letter is in its Vaikhari form, the gross manifestation of sound within.The physical sacral plexus corresponds to this Lotus. Within the Lotus, there is a quadrangular Mandal which is the symbol of a perfect creation, the Earth element (Prithvi Tattva), and secret occult power. The seed Letter of this element is LAM (the shining protector of the world), it is also the Bij of Indra, Lord of Celestials, seated on his seven-tusked Elephant Airavata, a symbol of strength, firmness, and solidity.

This Chakra corresponds to the Bhuloka or the Physical plane, region of the earth, abode of man, animals, vegetables, and minerals. The vital air working in this region is the Apana Vayu. The Guna or quality is Tamasic (inertia). Ganesha or Ganapati is the Deity of this Chakra; he is the great remover of obstacles, Lord of knowledge and intelligence and spiritual wealth. The Dakini Shakti presides over the Asthidhatu (bone). This Chakra commands the Padendriya (feet), Gamana Kriya (walking), Gandha (smell), Ghrana (nose). It is Nivrittikala (the aspect of renunciation).

There is first a preliminary verse immediately followed by three verses of introduction. Then begins strictly speaking study of the six Chakras (sat means six) of the subtle human body, and finally that of the Sahasrar Chakra which is at the top of the head and slightly outside the skull.

अथ तन्त्रानुसारेण षट् चक्रादि क्रमोद्गतः ।
उच्यते परमानन्द निर्वाह् प्रथमान्कुरः ॥

Atha tantranusarena sat Chakradi kramodgatah
Ucyate paramananda nirvaha prathamankurah

"now the author of the Sat Chakra Nirupan speaks of (the first step) sprouting shoot of the Yogi plant of complete realization of the Brahman, which is to be achieved, according to the Tantras, utilizing the six Chakras and so forth in their proper order" Preliminary verse – sat Chakra Nirupanam

मेरोर्बाह्यप्रदेशे शशि मिहिरशिरे सव्यदक्षे निषण्णे
मध्ये नाडी सुषुम्णात्रितयगुण्मयी चन्द्रसूर्यग्निरुपा
धत्तुरस्मेरपुष्प-ग्रथित-तमवपु: कन्दमध्यच्छिरःस्था
वज्राख्या मेढ्रदेशच्छिरसि परिगता मधमेऽस्या ज्वलन्ति ||१||

Merobahyapradeshe sasi mihirasire savyadakse nisanne
Madhye Nadi susumantritaya – gunamayi candrasuryagnirupa
Daattura – smera – puspagrathita – tamavapuh kandamadyacchirahstha
Vajrakhya medhradesachhirasi parigata madhame sya jvalanti

" In the space outside the meru , placed on the left and the right, are two Nadis (Ida – moon, and Pingala – sun). The Susumna Nadi, whose substance is the threefold Gunas, is in the middle. She is the form of the moon, Sun, and Fire. Like a string of blooming Dhatura flowers, extends from the middle of the kanda to the Head, and the Vajra inside Her extends, shining, from the medhra to the Head" Verse 1 – Sat Chakra Nirupanam

Here is the mention of Nadis and Chakras, the knowledge of which is necessary for Kundalini Yoga. Meru is literally a mountain, the central pole of the world. This is also the Sri Yantra. Likewise, Meru is the vertebral column of the human body. Ida and Pingla Nadis (the moon and the sun) are on left and the right side. Gunas refer to the qualities of the central Susumna Nadi as Satva, Rajas and Tamas. Susumna Nadi (tamas Guna) consists of the substance of the spinal cord (fiery red) within which there are three tubes, tube within tubes. From outside to inside is vajra Nadi, the outside canal (lustrous like the Sun, Rajas Guna), CitriniNadi, the middle canal (pale like the moon, Sattva Guna) and Brahma Nadi, the central canal.

तन्मध्ये चित्रिणी सा प्रणव विलासिता योगिनां योगगम्या
लूतातन्तुपमेया सकलसरसिजान मेरुमध्यान्तरस्थान
भित्त्वा देदीप्यते तद्ग्रन्थनरचनया शुद्ध- बोध - स्वरुपा
तन्मध्ये ब्रह्मनाडी हरमुख कुहरदादिदेवान्तसंस्था || २ ||

Tanmadhye citrini sa pranavavilasita yoginam yogagamya
Lutatantupameya sakalasarasijan merumadhyantarasthan bhitva dedipyate tad – grathanaracanaya suddha – bodh- svarupa
Tanmadhye brahmaNadi haramukha kuharaddi – devan sanstha

"Inside her is Citrini, who is lustrous with the lustre of the Pranava and attainable by Yogis in Yoga. Citrini is pure intelligence and subtle like a spider's thread, pierces all the Lotuses which are placed along the backbone. She is beautiful by reason of these lotuses which are strung on Her. Within Citrini is the Brahma Nadi, the innermost duct of Susumna and the Nadi through which Kundalini goesfrom Muladhara to Parama Shiva , which extends from the orifice of the mouth of Hara (the orifice at the top of the svayambhu Linga in the Muladhara) to the place beyond where is Adi Deva (the supreme bindu) "Verse 3 – Sat Chakra Nirupanam

विदयुन्माला - विलासा मुनिमनसिलसततन्तरूपा सुसूक्ष्मा
शुद्धज्ञानप्रबोधा सकलसुखमयी शुद्धबोधस्वभावा।
ब्रह्मद्वारं तदायते प्रविलसति सुधाधारगम्यप्रदेशं
ग्रन्थिस्थानं तदेतद् वदनमिति सुषुम्णाख्यनाड्या लपन्ति॥

"Citrini (or Citra Nadi) is beautiful like a chain of lightning (the Chakras) and fine like a lotus fibre. She shines in the mind of Yogis. She is extremely subtle, the awakener of pure knowledge and the embodiment of all Bliss, whose true nature is pure Consciousness. The Brahmadvara shines in her mouth. The place in the entrance of the region sprinkled by ambrosia is called the Knot (Granthi – Sthanam), or the mouth of Susumna" Verse 3 – Sat Chakra Nirupanam

Let us now begin with the study of each Chakra, beginning with Muladhara upto the Svadhisthan, and then the Manipur, the Anahat, the Visuddhi Ajna and the last Sahasrar, and concluding with an evocation of the Kundalini powers. One must understand that the language used here is adapted to very subtle and complex apparatuses, not visible by the human physical eyes and difficult to be accepted by the modern science...although it is there. All Tantric means aim at awakening these subtle and still more subtle potentials.

MuladharaChakra increases the intellect and the ability to write. It leads to the knowledge of the past, the present and the future and the knowledge of the scriptures. It destroys and thus leads to the natural bliss of Samadhi and the control of Prana, the mind and semen. It gives also the power to rise from the ground (Darduri Siddhi).

Regarding the placing of the deities in the Muladhara Chakra, two schools of practice are available, slightly differing from each other. The Rudra Yamala and Sat Chakra Nirupan place Brahma in the Muladhara, along with Indraand Dakini (queen of Muladhara) as the Yogini, then Kamarupa and Kandarpa Vayu Apana. The Mulatrikona the triple Shakti of Iccha (will, desire – sristi), Kriya (action, movement – Sthithi), and Jnana (knowledge – Samhara), and the three Goddesses Vama (Brahmi), Jyestha (Vaisnavi) and Raudri (Sambhavi). In the middle of it is the Svayambhu Linga, the Panchavaktra Shiva (five-eyed Shiva), the Vaikhari state of sound (earthly sound, articulated sound).

Earth (with all solids) is the element, Lam is the Bija, Indra`s elephant Airavata the vehicle and Vajra (thunderbolt) the weapon. Here, the Kundalini is Cit Kala, Nityananda, Nirguna. This Chakra looks like the Bandhujiva flower of love, it corresponds to a part of the Bhupura of the Sri Yantra. The Ganesha Atharva Sirsa says: 'Tvam Muladharaasthito`si nityam, tvam sakti trayatmakah 'Sri Vidya keeps Ganapati as the Mula deity of the Chakra.The remover of obstacle – Ganapati could be identified with the Brahmanaspati of the Vedas. Among the body parts, he represents the anus and the nose and smell (Gandha) is the Tanmatra. Red and crimson are his colours, his Nadi is alambusa, his tissues are muscles and flesh, Dosa is Kapha and Vayu Apana.

The four petals represent the four Vedas:

1 वं Vam Varadayai Namah

2 शं Sam sriyai Namah

3 षं Sam Sndayai Namah

4 सं Sam Sarasvatyai Namah

Asthi Dhatu is the tissue related to the Earth, the solid element. Dakini protects it as a Yogini – while in Sri Vidya we call her Sakini. The Rudra Yamala gives Brahma to open the Brahmagranthi with Mantras, it is the seventh Chakrabedhan (opening or piercing of the Chakras). It gives also Kundalini Kavach and Kundalini Sahasranam. Great stress is also given in this Rudra Yamala Tantra about Kumari worship with Kavaca and Sahasranam. Kumari represents Bala Tripurasundari, the root vidya of Sri Vidya, Trayaksari (like the Kundalini Bija which is also Trayaksari). Sri Vidya also gives a very detailed worship of Ganesha with Mantra, Gayatri, stotra, kavach and Sahasranam.

In Sri Vidya, we don't aim only at awakening the Kundalini, but learn the art and science of worshipping her and expanding her power and consciousness. Tripurasundari is the Kundalini, the Empress of the universe. We have to approach her gradually, both at the physical and universal plane. Ganapati, Batuk and Bala are child deities, preparing us with milder energies to merge into higher energies levels of consciousness leading to the Ultimate. Brahma sitting on the swan is the symbol of the Hamsah. Hamsa is the form of the Mantra in Muladhara. It is the starting point of the Hamsa Vidya. Ugratara is the mahavidya linked to Muladhara. Adrenals are the endocrine glands connected to Muladhara.

सां हंस:Muladhara Adhistan devatayai Sakini sahit gananath svarupinyai namah

In brief, Muladhara is a lotus of four red petals having on them gold letter Vam, Shham, Sham and sam. In the pericarp is the Adhara - Mandala with eight spears and in the lower part is the Adhara - Bija (Lam) who has four arms and is seated on the elephant Airavata. He is yellow and holds Vajra (thunderbolt) in his hands. Inside the Bindu of Adhara - Bija is the four-faced child Brahma who is red in color and has four hands with Danda (staff), Kamandalu (Gourd), Rudraksha Rosary and Abhaya Mudra (fearless seal) . in the pericarp besides Brahma is a red lotus on which is seated a red - colored and four armed Shakti Dakini , the presiding deity of the Chakra , holding Sula (spear) , Khatvanga (skull - mounted staff) , Khadga (sword) and Casak (drinking cup). In the pericarp is a lightning - like triangle inside which are Kama - vayu and Kama - Bija, both of which are red. Above this is the black Svayambhu LInga. Above and around this Linga is the Kundalini, coiled three and half times and above this last up stand. Cit - Kala on the top of Linga.

Within the Yellow square is a red triangle with an apex downwards called Yoni or Trikona, Tripura (Fire, sun, moon). It is the Shaktipitha *(*Abode of Shakti). It represents the triple aspect of Shakti, Iccha (will), Kriya (action), Jnana (knowledge), Kali, Lakshmi, Saraswati, Sristi (creation), Sthiti (maintenance), Samhara (destruction) the three Gunas : Sattva (purity), Rajas (activity) and Tamas (inertia).

The red color of the triangle represents the feminine energy (Shakti), the symbol of the Rajas hidden in the Yoni-sthan of the perineum muscle. Within the triangle is the Svayambhu Linga with the shape of a tender leaf. Svambhu means self-born; the Linga is the symbol of Shiva or Sukra (semen). The Svayambhu Linga is the reflecting consciousness as Chitta (Mind stuff, or subconscious mind); around it lies the Kundalini coiled up in three and half round representing the four states : Jagrat (waking), Svapna (dreaming), Sushupti (deep sleep) and the half round represents the fourth state of Turya (self-awareness). The two symbols of the Yoni and Linga are the ~~root~~ of spiritual practice. The Dhyan Bindu Upanishad says: "Bindu is Shiva, Rajas is Shakti, the combination of both is very difficult, through their union only the highest stage namely of Soma is achieved. "Swami Vishnu Tirth further explains: "A Yogi through Brahmacharya (continence), inverts the outflow of his semen and converts it into Soma and thus acquires, control over the astral body. In the first stage, semen is sacrificed into the fire of the opposite sexual fluid situated in the muscle between the anus and the genital organ. When the two charges unite with (Kandarpa vayu), heat is produced which converts semen into a finer substance absorbed and purified by the gastric fire, then it moves to the heart creating a kind of electricity which later rises through the spine and gets stored up in the brain as Ojas Shakti or Soma, which brings control over mind, concentration, Prana and Astral body".

The Moolaadhar Chakra is the abode of the Brahma Granthi (the knot of Brahma), Brahma is the Divinity of creation, presiding over sexual desire. When the Kundalini is awakened it has to pierce this Knot made up of physio-vital desires which prevent and block our consciousness from evolving to higher states. Through the process of urdhvareta (sex sublimation, transformation) Yogis are gradually freed from Lust. As the Kundalini Upanishad says:

"Chitta (subconscious) is formed out of water."

"Chitta has two causes for its existence, Vasanas or subtle desires and the vibration of Prana (vital force)".

Concentration and Meditation on this chakra bring a perfect knowledge of the Kundalini. And the techniques to awaken her are the Mulabandha (the downward vital air Apana forced to move upward by the contraction of the sphincter muscles of the anus), Saraswati and Shakti Chalan, etc.;

To gain mastery over this Chakra 600 repetitions of the SO HAM HAM SAH mantra are required during 24 Hours. The full development of the Mooladhar brings, knowledge of the earth and the physical world. It increases the intellect, the ability to write, it leads to the Knowledge of the past, present and future, the

Knowledge of the scriptures; it destroys sins, leads to natural bliss of Samadhi and the control of Prana, Mind and semen; power to rise from the ground (Darduri Siddhi).

(2) THE SVADHISHTHANA CHAKRA

(Illustration by Swami Jayramdas)

The svadhisthan Chakra is above the genitals. On it's six petals are the letters from Ba to Purandar (the Lam Matrak, of the shining color of lightning with the Bindu superimposed. Verse 14 Sat Chakra Nirupan.

तस्याङ्कदेशकलितो हरिरेव पायात्
नीलप्रकाश रुचिरश्रियमादधानः ।
पीताम्बरः प्रथमयौवनगर्वधारी
श्रीवत्सकौस्तुभधरो धृतवेदबाहुः ||१६||

Tasyankadesakaliko harireva payat
Nila prakasarucirasriyamadadhanah
Pitambarah prathamayauvana garvadhari
Srivatsa kaustubhadharo dhrtavedabahuh ||१६||

"within it is the white, watery region of Varuna, of the shape of a half - moon and therein, seated on a Makara, is the Bija Vam, stainless and white as the autumnal Moon." Verse 15 Sat Chakra Nirupanam.

" may Hari, who is within the lap of the Bindu of Yam, who is in the pride of early youth, whose body is of a luminous blue beautiful to behold, who is dressed in yellow raiment and who is four armed and wears the Srivastsa, the favourite of Sri or Laksmi (this is the auspicious curl of hair on the chest of Visnu and His Avtar Krsna which symbolises Prakrti, the world of matter) and the Kaustubh (a divine jewel which is in the possession of Lord Visnu and who lives in Ksir Sagar, the ocean of milk), May Hari protect us !" Verse 16 Sat Chakra Nirupanam.

अत्रैवभाति सततं खलुराकिणि सा
नीलाम्बुजोदरसहोदर कान्तिशोभा
नानायुधोदयतकरैर्लसितानगलक्ष्मी
दिव्याम्बराभरणभूषितमत्तचित्ता || १७ ||

Atraiva bhati satatam khalu rakini sa
Nilambujo darasahodar kanti shobha
Nanayudhodyata kararlasitanga laksmir
Divyambara bharana bhusitamatta citta|| १७||

It is here that Rakini always dwells. She is of the color of a blue lotus. The beauty of Her Body enhanced by Her uplifted arms holding various weapons. She is dressed in celestial raiment and ornaments and Her mind is exalted with the drinking of ambrosia. Verse 17 Sat Chakra Nirupanam.

स्वधिष्ठानाख्यमेतत्सरसिजममलं चिन्तयेद् यो मनुष्य-
स्तस्याऽहन्कारदोषादिकसकलरिपुः श्रीयते तत्क्षणेन
योगीशः सोडपिमोहअद्द्भुततिमिरचये भानुतुल्यप्रकाशो
गदयैःपदयैः प्रबन्धैर्विरचयति सुधावाक्यसन्दोह्लक्ष्मीः ||१८||

Svadhisthanakhyam etat sarasijamamalam cintayedyo manusya
Stasyahamkara dosadika sakala ripuh ksiyate tatksanena
Yogisah so pimohad bhutatimiracaye bhanu tulya prakaso
Gadyaih padyaih parabhandhair viracayati sudhavaky
asandoha lakshmih ||१८||

"he who meditates upon this stainless lotus which is named svadhisthan is immediately freed from all his enemies such as the fault of Ahamkara and so forth. He becomes lord among Yogis and is like the sun illumining the dense darkness of ignorance. The wealth is his nectar - like words flow in rose and verse in well - reasoned discourse." Verse 18 Sat Chakra Nirupanam.

Next above at the root of the genitals we find the Svadhishthana Chakra. Unlike the Mooladhar which was at the root of the Sushumna Nadi, this chakra abides within the Sushmna.

This Lotus is of vermiliom colour (sindur) and is the origin of the urge for procreation. It derives its meaning from Sva (Param Lingam); Svadhishthana means "good standing place", well positioned. It has six petals formed by the position of the Nadis at this level. These Nadis produce vibrations which are represented by six Sanskrit letters having the colour of lightning.

BAM meaning good looking, destroyer of all bad habits. BHAM destroyer of all evil sprits.

MAM the hypnotiser of all the opponents.

YAM The all-pervading sanctifier.

RAM The seed letter of Fire

LAM The shining protector of the world.

The six petals represent the six Vrittis (states, mental modifications, inclinations) Prasraya (credulity), (2) Avishvasa (suspicion, mistrust), (3) Avajna (disdain), (4) Murccha (delusion, disinclination) (5) Sarvanasa (false knowledge), (6) Krurata (pitilessness). The figure six, is expressed by the Hexgone, the balance between water and fire, the opposition of good and evil; it is often a symbol of sin. This Chakra corresponds to the Bhuvar Loka, the sphere situated between the earth and the sun (Kama loka, the sphere of desire). It rules the lower vital being, which is ignorant, made up of obscure desires, passions, revolts, which never cease to rise from the subconscious. It corresponds in the physical body to the prostatic plexus. It has control over the lower abdomen, the kidneys, prostate, etc...

The ruling element of this plexus is water *(*Apas, Jal Mandal). It symbolizes life creation, purification but also dissolution and the fluidity of Vital desires. Apana is the vital air working at this level; its quality (guna) is Rajasic (activity). Within the lotus is a space resembling, a white crescent moon, symbol of chastity and birth, day and night passivity, femineity. The seed letter of this chakra is VAM (pure water), it is the bij of Varuna, the deity of the ocean; it stands in the Sushumna. He is seated on a white Makara a kind of water monster derived from the crocodile and the dolphin.

This animal corresponds to the winter solstice, the ascend ing course of the sun propitious for spiritual practice; it is the gate of the Gods, the solar gate. It also represents both liberation and destruction, comparable with the lower vital being, who liberates when controlled, and destroys spiritual evolution when deluding. The ear rings of Vishnu represent Makaras, symbol of intellectual knowledge and intuition. This monster is a lunar and night symbol, its position between the earth and water element, represents fundamental contradictions, fecundity, and vicious demoniac nature. The Kundalini's motion at this level is like the monster, clumsy on the ground, fast in waters. Varuna is an old Vedic divinity. The word means source of bliss, most venerable, chosen one. He is described as the benevolent God, into whose palate flew the seven rivers as into a hollow channel. He creates heaven, earth, and the intermediate space.

The Deity of this chakra is Brahma (the creator) which sprang out of Vishnu's navel on a lotus. He symbolizes the Rajas quality (expensive) with his Shakti Savitri. He is the Lord of creation, the prompter of spiritual evolution, cosmic intelligence. In his guiding form he created the means for further progress. The Devi Rakini presides over the Raktadhatu (blood). The Svadishthana is the centre of Taste (rasa tattva), it controls the organ of grasping (pani). Here consciousness belongs to the dream state (taijasa) and sound to the Pashyanti state.

For mastery of this Plexus 6000 repetitions of the SO HAM HAM SAH mantra are required during 24 hours. Concentration and meditation on this chakra bring control over the water element or the powers of transformation, and control over material desires, intuitional knowledge, telepathy, knowledge of the astral entities, control over the senses. It destroys impure qualities, and develops psychic powers. Therefore, Yogis become vanquishers of Death like Lord Shiva (Maha Mrityunjaya). However, this Chakra, like the Mooladhar must be crossed quickly by the seekers, their piercing creates heat and (momentarily) increases sexual urge.

The Sat Chakra Nirupan gives the Bhuvansvar Dhyan, Sva means Paralinga. The elements is water (ambhoja Mandalam), Deity is varuna and vehicle is Crocodile. The shape of this Chakra is like half-moon. Varuna is four armed and blue coloured. Visnu is within the lap of Bindu. He wears the Srivatsa mark, the favourite of Laksmi.

There is a meditation on this dark blue Visnu with mace representing mahat Adi Buddhi, the universal intelligence, cosmic intelligence. Visnu is seated on Garuda. The conch symbolizes the sattvic Ahmkara (illumination or enlightening knowledge) while the bow is the tamasic Ahamkara, the sword is the Divine Knowledge, the discus the mind and the arrow the senses. The abode is the self, Vam is the Bija and the symbol is a white crescent moon. Sense organ is the tongue, gonads and testes are the endocrine glands, water is the element, taste the Tanmatra, vermilion the color, kuhu the Nadi, fat the tissue, Kapha the Dosa and Apana is the Vayu (or Prana, vital air). Both Rudra Yamala and Sat Chakra nirupan give the same description. The Rudra yamala gives a beautiful Krsna Sahasranam along with the Rakini Sahasranam – here, Rakini is the Yogini protecting the Medha Dhatu (fat). In Sri Vidya, it is called Kakini, who has a furious aspect with spear, lotus, drum and battle axe in hands.

The Bija is moon – while Vam located in the innermost centre of the Chakra

1 वं Vam Varunaya Namah

It has six vermilion – colored petals representing different Vrttis:

2 बं Bam Bandhinyai Namah

3 भं Bham Bhadrakalyai Namah

4 मं Mam Mayayai Namah

5 यं Yam Yasasvinyai Namah

6 रं Ram Raktayai Namah

7 लं Lam lambostyai Namah

कां सोऽहं

Svadhistan Adhistan Devatayai kakini Sahit Brahma svarupinyai Namah

Meditation on Svadhisthan frees from all enemies. One becomes Lord among the Yogis. Rakini Kavaca, mantra and Sahasranam are given in the Rudra Yamala, along with Sri krsna`s Bhuvanesvari (or Bala) is the Maha Vidya linked to the Svadhisthan Chakra. Soham is the form of the Mantra at this stage. To summarize, Svadhisthan Chakra, of vermilion color, has six letters (Bam, Bham, Mam, Yam, Ram, Lam) of the color of lightning placed on the petals. In the pericarp of the main lotus, there is a white region with a second eight – petalled lotus with half – moon in its centre. Inside the region is the Varuna – Bija, Vam, seated on a Makaara and with noose on hand. In the hollow of the Bindu is Visnu sitting on Garuda and holding in His four hands the conch, the mace and the Lotus. Visnu, full of youth and pride, wears yellow raiment, a garland of forest flowers, the mark of Srivatsa on his chest and a gem kaustubh on His Breast. Fierce looking Rakini Sakti with three eyes and Syama Varna (dark complexion) , projecting fangs and bleeding nostrils, sits in the pericarp of the red lotus and holds in her four hands Sula, Abja, Damaru and Tanaka (spear , lotus , drum and battle-axe). She is fond of white rice.

(3) THE MANIPURA CHAKRA

(Illustration by Swami Jayramdas)

The Manipura chakra is the third plexus located within the Sushumna at the centre of the navel region, hence the name Mani Padma of dark hue like the heavy-laden rain clouds. It corresponds to the Solar plexus in the physical body and has control over the liver, stomach etc... It is very important for the functioning of the body; a child in the womb is connected to the mother through the umbilical cord attached near this centre and is fed from there only. Yogis believe that during the astral journey the physical and astral body remain attached to each other by the subtle cord coming out through this centre. The cord is silvery, shining like a diamond (Mani) and this chakra is its city (Pura). It is also often referred as the Abdominal brain, the central storage of vital energy (Prana). The navel lotus is the seat of the dynamic vital consciousness, or higher vital being. The consciousness of the surface vital being is very narrow, ignorant, filled up with passions, obscure desires, revolts, dualities (pain, pleasure) depression; it is extremely change able and influenced by the subconscious state. But behind that surface consciousness there is a true vital being which is vast, peaceful, strong, unlimited firm and very potent. It is a projection and an instrument of the God Head, like the sattvik Avatar of RAM, infinite power of spiritual evolution. This Chakra corresponds to Svar Loka, the sphere situated between the Sun and the Polar star an Abode of bliss and progression on the Yogic path. It is also known as Uru Loka, the wide other world. Svar Loka is of supercelestial wideness, the one of illimitable light of truth, transcendental heaven of bliss.

The Manipura Chakra has ten petals of purple like colour. The figure ten represent the return to unity, universal creation, the sum of the two previous chakras. On the petals we find the ten Vritti (mental modifications of consciousness) (1) Lajja (shame), Pisunata (fickleness), 3 Irsha (jealousy), 4 Trishna (desire) 5 Sushupti (laziness), 6 Vishada (sadness), 7 Kashaya (dullness), 8 Moha (attachment) 9 Ghrina (disgust, aversion) and 10 Bhaya (fear).

On the petals we find, produced by the vibrations of the Nadis the blue Sanskrit letters:

DAM the antidote for poisons, DHAM the fortune giver, NAM the giver of siddhis, TAM the joyful giver of all fortunes, THAM the pure, producer of virtues, NAM the peaceful giver of enjoyments and moksha. PAM the destroyer of obstacles in the shape of poisons and PHAM the shinning, giver of Animadi siddis. These letters vibrate in the solar Pingala Nadi.

Within the pericarp we find a red triangular figure (Mandal of Agni), Lord of Fire, the figure is surrounded on each side by an auspicious Svastika. This chakra is the abode of Tejas Tattwa (fire element), Rajo Guna (activity) and the Samana vital air. (Working for digestion). The red triangle with apex downwards symbolizes the triple aspect of fire (1) Agni (earthly fire), Indra (lightning), 3 Surya (celestial fire). 1 Bhaumagni (earthly fire), 2 Divyagni (celestial fire), 3 Jatharagni (the stomachal fire or Vaishvanara produced in the stomach by digestion. It is also Ahavaniya, the sacrificial fire produced by the union of the Prana and Apana vital airs at this level.

The three Svastikas represent auspiciousness, rotation, a constant regeneration and motion.

The ten petals also represent the ten Kalas (aspects) of fire.

(1) Bhrajaka (shining)

(2) Ranjaka (colouring, rejoicing)

(3) Kledaka (which brings perspiration)

(4) Snehaka (which loves, affectionate)

(5) Dharaka (which sustains)

(6) Bandhaka (which holds, ties)

(7) Dravaka (which melts, brings passions)

(8) Vyapaka (which penetrates all)

(9) Mapaka (which measures, regulates)

(10) Shleshmaka (which surrounds)

RAM is the seed letter of this lotus, the bij of Fire; it vibrates in the Sushumna; within the triangle, he is seated on a Ram, which is a cosmic representation of the animal power of fire, creative and destructive. It is the primary vitality of life, instinct. The Ram is also the vehicle of Kubera, the Lord of riches. At this level the motion of the Kundalini resembles that of the Ram. The presiding. Deity of the chakra is Lord Vishnu with the Goddess Laxmi, who represents maintenance in life, a constant positive source of energy and blessings, spiritual wealth.

The four-armed Lakini Shakti presides over the Mamsadhatu (flesh). Above the lotus is the abode and region of Surya, the solar region absorbing nectar which drops from the Lunar region of the palate. The three plexuses, Mooladhar, Svadhishthana, Manipura preside over the function of the physical body (Virat). The Pashyanti aspect of sound ends at this chakra. Rupa is the Tanmatra (subtle fire). Chakshu (eyes) is the organ of Knowledge presided by the sun and Payu (anus) the organ of action is presided by Mrityu (lord of death). Con centration and meditation on this chakra bring control over life and death. "In the navel circle comes the knowledge of the constitution of the body." Pat, Yoga sutra: III. 30.

ध्यायेन्मेषाधिरुढंनवतपननिभं वेदबाहूज्ज्वलाङ्गं
तत्क्रोडे रुद्रमूर्तिर्निवसति सततं शुद्धसिन्दूररागः
भस्मालिप्ताङ्गभूषाभरणसितवपुर्वृद्धरूपी त्रिनेत्रो
लोकनामिष्टदाताऽभयलसितकरः सृष्टिसंहारकारी ||२०||

Dhyayen mesadhirudham navatapanaanibham vedabahuj jvalangam
Tat – korde rudra murtirnirvasti satatam suddhasinduraragah

Bhasma liptanga bhusa bharanasaita vapor vrddharupi trinentro
Loka namistadata bhayala sitakarah sristi samharakari||२०||

"Meditate upon him (Vahni, Fire) seated on a ram, four armed, radiant like the rising Sun. in His lap over dwells Rudra, who is of a pure vermilion hue. He (Rudra) is white with the ashes with which he is smeared, of an ancient aspect and three - eyed. His hands are placed in the attitude of granting boons and dispelling fear. He is the destroyer of Creation." Verse 20 sat Chakra Nirupan

अत्रास्ते लाकिनी सा सकलशुभकारी वेदबाहुज्वलाङ्गी
श्यामा पीताम्बराद्यैर्विविधविरचनालङ्कृता मत्तचित्ता
ध्यात्वैतन्नाभिपद्मं प्रभवति नितरां संहृतौ पालने वा
वाणी तस्याननाब्जे निवसति सततं ज्ञानसन्दोहलक्ष्मीः ||२१||

Atrate lakini sa sakalasubhamkari vedabahuj jvalangi
Syama pitambaradyair vividha viracanalam krta mattacitta
Dhya tvai tannabhi padmam prabhavati nitaram samhrtau palane va
Vani tasyananabje nivasati satatam jnana samdoha laksmi ||२१||

"here abides laksmi , the benefactress of all. She is four armed, of radiant body, dark of complexion, clothed in yellow raiment, decked with various ornaments and exalted with the drinking ambrosia. By meditating on this navel Lotus, the power to destroy and create (the world) is acquired. Vani (Sarasvati) with all the wealth of knowledge ever abides in the Lotus of His face. " Verse 21 sat Chakra Nirupanam

The Manipur Chakra is the third plexus. It is again within the Susumna and at the centre of the navel region, hence the name Mani Padma. It is of dark hue, like the heavy-laden rain clouds. In the physical body, it corresponds to the solar plexus and has control over the liver, the stomach. Manipur also means the city of jewels, lustrous like a gem. Daksina kalika is the Mahavidya with Batuk Bhairav, the child Shiva. It is the region of fire.

The Bij is Ram

रं Ram Raktayai Namah

Rudra is the deity, sitting on a ram, the body smeared with ashes. Eye is the sense organ, motor organs are the feet and Tanmatra the sight. It is dark blue. Nadi is Visvodhar, tissues are blood and flesh (Rakta and Mamsa Dhatu), Dosa is Pitta, Vayu is Samana and pancreas is the endocrine gland. Lakini is the Yogini presiding and protecting, she is the benefactress of all. She is four armed, radiant, of a dark blue complexion , three faced , three eyed. Here, the yogini is the same as in Sri Vidya.

The Chakra has ten petals

1	डम	Dam Damryai Namah
2	ढम	Dham Dhankarinyai Namah
3	नम	Nam Narnayai Namah
4	तं	Tam Tamasyai Namah
5	थं	ThamSthanavyai Namah
6	दं	Dam Dakayanyai Namah

7	धं	Dham Dhatrayai Namah
8	नं	Nam Naryai Namah
9	पं	Pam Parvatyai Namah
10	फ़म्	Pham Phatkarinyai Namah

The Rudra Yamala gives the Lakini Mantra, Kavaca and sahasranam, along with the Mrutyanjaya's. Rupa (form) is the Tattva, sight is the sense organ and feet the motor organ.

" Hamsah So Ham " is the mantra at this level (according to Sri Vidya , the Mantras Hamsah So Ham has special sequence for each Chakra. It means an ascendant progression, like the different scales in term of music.

लां हंसस्सोऽहं

Manipur adhisthan Devatayai kakini sahit vishnusvarupinyai namah

To sum up, the Nabhi Padma (navel lotus) is rain – cloud coloured with ten lustrous blue petals having the letters, Dam, dham, Nam, Tam, Tham, Dam, Dham, Nam, Pam on them and with the Bindu above each of them. Triangular – shaped red region of Fire with Svastika signs on its three sides is in the pericarp, within which is the four – armed Bija of Fire, Ram, which is red in color, seated on a ram, holding in His hands the Vajra (thunderbolt) and the Sakti weapons and making the Mudra of vara and Abhaya. Rudra, red in color, sits on a bull on the lap of Vahni – Bija. She is blue, four armed, three faced with three eyes on each face, she holds the Vajra and shakti weapons in her two hands and makes Abhaya and Vara Mudra with the other two hands. She is fierce with protruding teeth, is fond of eating cooked Rice and dahl mixed with meat and blood.

(4) THE ANAHATA CHAKRA

(Illustration by Swami Jayramdas)

Anahat Chakra

"Above that in the heart is the Anahat Chakra carries Lotus, of the shining color of the Bandhuka Flower, with the twelve letters beginning with Ka, of the color of vermilion, placed therein. It is known by the name of Anahat and is like the celestial withing – tree, bestowing even more than the supplicant`s desire. The region of Vayu which is like unto the smoke in color, beautiful and six corners, is here. " Versa 22 sat Chakra Nirupanam

तन्मध्ये पवनाक्षरञ्च मधुरं धूमावलीधूसरं
ध्यायेत्पाणिचतुष्टयेन लसितं कृष्णाधिरुढं परं
तन्मध्ये करुणानिधानममलं हंसाभमीशाभिधं
पाणिभ्यामभयं वरञ्च विदधल्लोकत्रयाणामपि || 23 ||

Tanmadhye pavanaksaram ca madurm dhumavalidhusarm
Dhyayet panicatustayena lasitam krsna dhirudham param
Tanmadhye karunanid namamalam hamsa bhamisabhidham
Pani bhyamabhayam varam ca vidadhal – lokatrayanamapi || 23 ||

"Meditate within it on the sweet and excellent Pavana Bija, grey as a mass of smoke, with four arms and seated on a black antelop. And within it also meditate upon the abode of mercy, the stainless Lord who is lustrous like the Sun, and whose two hands make the gestures which grant boons and dispels the fears of three world." Versa 23 sat Chakra Nirupanam

अत्रास्ते खलु काकिनी नवतत्पितात्रिनेत्रा शुभा
सर्वालङ्कारणान्विता हितकारी सम्यग्जनानां मुदा
हस्तैः पाशकपालशोभनवरान् सम्बिभ्रति चाभयं
मत्ता पूर्णासुधारसार्द्रहृदया कङ्कालमालाधरा ||२४||

Atraste khalu kakini navatatpita trinetraa subha
Sarvalamkarananvita hitakari samyag – janaanam muda

Hastaih pasakapala sobhanavaram sambhibhrati cabhayam
Matta purana sudharasaradra hrdaya kankala maladhara|| २४||

" Here dwell kakini, who is yellow in color like unto new lightning, exhilarated and auspicious, three eyed and the benefactress of all. She wears all kinds of ornaments and in her four hands carries the noose and the skull and make the sign of blessing and the sign which dispels fear. Her heart is softened with drinking of nectar." Versa 24 sat Chakra Nirupanam

एतन्नीरजकर्णिकान्तरलसच्छक्तिस्त्रिकोणाभिधा
विद्युत्कोकोटिसमानकोमलवपुः सास्ते तदन्तर्गतः
बाणाख्यः शिवलिङ्गकोऽपि कनकाकाराङ्गरागोज्ज्वलो
मौलौ सूक्ष्मविभेद्युङ् मणिरिव प्रोल्लासलक्ष्म्यालयः ||२५||

Etan niraja karnikantaralasac – chaktis triloka bhidha
Vidhyut koti samana komala vapuh saste tadantar gatah
Banakhyah Shivalinga ko pi kanaka karangargoj jvalo
Maualu sukshma vibhedayum maniriva prollasa laksmyalayah ||२५||

"The Sakti whose tender body is like ten million flashes of lightening is in the pericarp of this Lotus in the form of a triangle (Trilokanan). Inside the triangle is the Shiva – Linga known by the name Bana. This Linga is like shining gold and on his head is an orifice minute as that in a gem. He is the resplendent abode of Lakshmi." Versa 25 sat Chakra Nirupanam

ध्यायेयेद्यो हृदी पङ्कजं सुरतरु शर्वस्यपीठालयं
देवस्याऽनिल - हीन - दीप - कलिका - हंसेन संशोभितं ।
भानोर्मण्डल मणिदतान्तर लसत्किङ्जल्क शोभाधरं
वाचामीश्वरईश्वरोऽपि जगतां रक्षविनाशेक्षमः ||२६||

Dhyayedho hrdi pankajam suratarum sarvasya pithalayam
Devasyanila – hina – dipa – kalika – hamsena – samsobhitam
Bhanormandala – manditantara lasat kinjalka shobhadharam
Vacam isvara isvaro pi jagatam raksavinase ksamah|| २६||

" He who meditates on this Heart Lotus becomes like the Lord of Speech and like isvara he is able to protect and destroy the worlds. This lotus is like the celestial wishing – tree, the abode and seat Sarva. It is beautified by the Hamsah which is like unto the steady tapering flame of a lamp in windless place. The filaments which surrounds and adorn its pericarp, illuminied by the solar region, charm." Versa 26 sat Chakra Nirupanam

योगीशो भवति प्रियात्प्रियतमः कान्ताकुलस्याऽनिशं
ज्ञानीशोऽपि कृती जितेन्द्रियगणो ध्यानावधानक्षमः
गदयैः पद्यपदादिभिश्च सततंकाव्याम्बुधारावहो
लक्ष्मीरङ्गगणदैवतः पुरपुरे शक्तः प्रवेष्टुं क्षणात् ||२७||

Yogishobhavati priyatpriyatamah kantakulsyanisam
Jnaniso pi krti jitendriyagano dhyanavadhanksamah
Gadyaih padyapadadibhisca satatam kavyambhudharavaho
Lakshmiranganadaivatah parapure saktah pravestum ksanat ||२७||

Versa 27 sat Chakra Nirupanam

"Foremost among Yogis, he is ever dearer than the dearest to women. He is pre – eminently wise and full of noble deeds. His senses are completely under control. His mind in its intense concentration is engrossed in thoughts of the Brahman. His inspired speech flows like a stream of clear water. He is like the Devata who is beloved of laksmi and is able to enter another's body at will." Versa 27 sat Chakra Nirupanam

6000 srepetitions of the SO HAM HAM SAH mantra are required daily for the mastery of this plexus. Here Karmic results equal Karmic actions. In this chakra the karmic principle causes karmic results to ripen.

By mastery of this plexus, Yogis create psychic heat, obtain freedom from diseases, acquisition of hidden treasures, immunity from fire, patala siddhi. They become able to absorb more prana (vital force) and develop curing abilities. This chakra is also the seat of the Itara Linga (abode of manas, mind). At the navel level is performed the Uddiyana bandha, by drawing in the intestines and the navel towards the back. This leads the Prana through the Sushumna Nadi, removing impurities and diseases of the navel.

"By the conquest of the current Samana, he is surrounded by a blaze of light" Pat Yoga sutra: III. 41

The Anahata chakra is situated within the Sushumna Nadi, and corresponds to the cardiac plexus. The name Anahata is derived from the continuous sound which is heard by yogis at this level; it means unbeaten or unwound ed and refers to the sound OM, which is not produced by percussion. It is the spontaneous pulsation of life, the Shabda Brahman. Here sound is called Madyama and is associated with the intellect (buddhi). It corresponds to the mental movement, the dream state.

This chakra corresponds to Mahar Loka, the sphere going up the limits of our universe, dwelling abode of Saints and Munis. This plexus is usually divided into two parts, in front the Higher vital being, the emotive being and behind the psychic being, the soul. This chakra of the green air has twelve petals, produced by the position of the Nadis. The sound emanating from the Nadis is represented by vermillion Sanskrit letters:

KAM the propitious, antidote to all poisons.

KHAM the All, agitating

GAM the greatest remover of all obstacles.

GHAM the fortunate, the giver of stability.

NGAM the antidote for all deadly poisons.

CHAM the cruel, the destroyer of amenities.

CHHAM the greatest remover of evil spirits.

JAM the destroyer of black magic.

JHAM the destroyer of evil spirits.

JÑAM the conqueror of Death.

TAM the fortunate curer of all diseases.

THAM Lunar, svaha.

These letters vibrate in the Pingala Nadi (solar).

The figure 12 represents the twelve signs of the Zodiac, the twelve months of the year, the four elements: earth, water, fire and air, multiplied by the three qualities (gunas : tamas, rajas, sattva). It symbolizes the internal complexity of the universe, the end of a cycle.

In the twelve petals we find the twelve Vrittis (mental modification) (1) Asha (hope), 2 Chinta (anxiety), 3 Cesta (endeavour), 4 Mamata (mineness), 5 Dambha (arrogance), 6 Vikalata (langour), *7* Ahamkara (conceit), 8 viveka (discrimi nation), Lolata (covetousness), 10 Kapatata (duplicity), 11 Vitarka (indecision) 12 Anutapa (regret).

Within the lotus we find a Hexagon (shatkona), symbolizing spiritual aspiration and its responding grace, Shiva and Shakti. The triangle with the apex downwards represents Shakti, the Heart, femineity, water. The triangle with apex upwards represents, fire, Shiva. This hexagon has the colour of smoke; it is the seat of the Bana Linga, abode of Buddhi, Hiranyagarbha (intellect). Within the Hexagon is the seed letter of Air YAM, the all-pervading sanctifier, which vibrates within the Sushumna Nadi.

Vayu Tattva (air element) is also called Prana tattva; it is the mediator between all the other elements, its characteristics are lightness, movement, fluidity. It carries luminous rays, sound waves and perfumes. Air penetrates all the other Tattvas, it is at the root of Pranayama (control of the vital force); it is the source of life given to our body. Air is also the great purifier, the cosmic breath. It is a male and active principle like fire. It liberates, frees from earthly weight.

Vayu is the lord of cosmic vitality.

He is also known as Matarisvan, since it breathes in the atmosphere, or moves quickly in that region. Vayu is the protector of Soma (nectar); he knows and sustains everything. Vayu (air) is seated on a black antelope, symbol of velocity beauty, gracefulness, speed and emotivity. The motion of the Kundalini is here compared with this swift animal.

Ishwara (Shiva) is the deity of this Chakra with his Shakti Bhuvaneshwari. He is of the colour of molten gold. The Kakini Shakti, wearing a garland of Human bones presides over the Raktadhatu (blood). The quality of this chakra is a mixture of Rajas (activity) and Sattva (purity) The vital air working at this level is Prana. This Lotus is also the seat of the Vishnu Granthi, the knot of consciousness created by our vital and emotional being. The figure twelve also represents the twelve Yoginis adored here: Vidya Yogini, Rechika, Mochika, Amrita, Dipika, Jnana, Apyayani, Vyapini, Medha, Vyomarupa, Siddhi rupa, Lakshmi Yogini.

Sparsha (touch, subtle air) is the Tanmatra of this centre to which corresponds Tvak (sense of touch, presided by Vayu, dwelling is the skin) and Upastha (genitals) the organ of action presided by Prajapati. In this chakra the karmic principle causes karmic results to ripen. For the mastery of this chakra, 6000 repetitions of the SO HAM HAM SAH mantra are required during 24 hours.

रां हंसश्शिव स्सोऽहं

Anahat adhistan devatayai Rakini Sahit Sadashiva Svarupinyai namah. This is the evolution of the Hamsah Mantra.

Concentration and meditation on this chakra bring various types of material benefits, knowledge, the control of the air element, cosmic love, and many other sattvić qualities. Several psychic powers are also obtained like Bhuchari siddhi, Kechari siddhi, Kaya siddhi (flying in the air, entering other bodies) Patanjali Muni says: "In the heart, knowledge of minds" III. 35. However the Anahata Chakra is to be distinguished from the heart Chakra, Hriday Chakra also called Ananda Kanda, situated below it. It is a lotus of 8 petals often described in the Upanishads; it is the seat of the Ishtadevata (chosen deity). The Jewel altar (Manipitha) is installed under the tree granting all desires (kalpa vriksha).

The Dhyan Bindu Upanishad describes thus the Heart lotus:

"There is the Lotus of the heart with the flower down below and the stalk up above, facing downwards like the plantain flower replete with all the Veda, auspicious, enduring for a century, rich with a hundred petals and graceful like the full-blown lotus flower.

There should he conceive of the regions of the Sun, Moon and Fire, one over the other. In the middle of fire is lustre, in the middle of lustre is the seat surrounded with various gems. One should dutifully meditate upon Maha Vishnu in the middle of that seat, devoid of impurity, who is clear as the clearest crystal, resplendent like myriads of moons."

The Heart Lotus is also described as the seat of the Jivatman (incarnated soul), the "Hamsah". "In the seat of the heart, there is the eight petalled lotus; in the middle of it there is the form of the Jivatman, radiant having the size of a speck." "When it reposes in the eastern petal of white colour with devotion moving in front, there is an inclination towards (dharma) right conduct.

When it reposes in the south eastern petal of blood red colour of Agni (fire), there is proneness to slumber and sloth. When it reposes in the southern petal of black colour of Yama (death) there is a leaning towards spite and anger (cruel deeds). When it reposes in the south western petal of Nirriti of blue color, there is a tendency on its part towards sinful action and violence. When it reposes in the north western petal of Vayu of the colour of emerald, there is inclination towards movement and detachment.

When it reposes in the northern petal of yellow colour of the moon, there is proneness towards the enjoyment of pleasure and sex attraction. When it reposes in the north eastern petal of Isana colour of Lapilazuli, there is a tendency towards munificence, compassion acquiring material wealth.

When there is leaning towards the joints of the petals there is the rousing of Vata (vital air), Pitta (bile) and Sleshma (phlegm) and the great maladies. When it stands at the centre, it knows all, dances, reads, creates bliss. Within it is a first circle of the colour of Bandhuka flower, the state of waking. In the pericarp the state of dreaming is of the colour of the indragopa insect. The third circle is of the colour of the ruby the state of sushupti (deep sleep). The fourth is the state of Turya. It becomes of the form of eternal consciousness (self-awareness). 93.1-93.13."

A beautiful meditation is also offered to us in the Guru Gita:

"Meditate on the divine form of the guru seated on the throne situated in the centre of the pericarp of the heart Lotus, shining like the crescent of the moon, holding the book of knowledge and making the mudra bestow the desired boon. He is clad in white garments, is besmeared with white paste adorned with garlands of white flowers and pearls. He is joyous and a treasure house of abundant grace. His Divine Shakti, seated on the left side of his lap." V. 91.

The Figure 8 of this Lotus again represents the mental modifications of consciousness, but also the 8 Siddhis (psychic powers) revolving around the central Self (Hamsah), the 8 Bhairavas (forms of Shiva) and the eight Nayikas (Shaktis). 8 represents also cosmic balance, the eight planets revolving around the sun, the eight cardinal points.

(5) THE VISHUDDHA CHAKRA

(Illustration by Swami Jayramdas)

The Vishuddha Chakra is situated within the Sushumna Nadi at the base of the throat (kantha mula) It is also called Bharatisthan (seat of the goddess of speech). It corresponds to the laryngeal plexus. This chakra is so called because the Jivatman has attained purity (vishuddha) at the sight of the "Hamsa" (self). It governs the mental being of expression and extroversion. This lotus corresponds to Janar Loka, the sphere beyond our Universe, where one gets freed from passion, where the mind is united to the intellect. This chakra has 16 petals of smoky blue colour, the vibrations produced by the Nadis are represented by the Sanskrit vowels of crimson colour.

AM the all pervading

AAM the force of attraction working universally.

IM the peaceful power of nourishment.

IIM the pure power of speech.

UM the essence of all powers.

UUM the unbearable power of expulsion.

RIM Disturbing agitation of mind.

RIIM the bright power of hypnotism.

LRM hypnotic influence creating hatred.

LRRM Hypnotic power.

EM the purest.

AIM the purest power of attracting all.

OM the ever-pure word, godhead.

AUM the attractive, embracing all words.

AM hypnotic influence on animals.

AHA the destroyer of death.

The vowels are Shakti's and add power to the consonants, they are Lunar.

A,1,U,RI,LRAM, vibrate in the Pingala Nadi.

AA, II, UU, RII, LRR, AHA vibrate in the Ida Nadi.

E, AI,O,AU, vibrate in the Sushumna Nadi.

The sixteen petals correspond to the *7* Musical notes: Nisada, Rsabha, Gandhara, Sadja, Madhyama, Dhaivata and Panchama and Venom in the eight petal. The Bijas, HUM, PHAT, VAUSAT, SVADHA, NAMAH and in the sixteenth petal Nectar (Amrita).

This Lotus has Ether *(*Akash) for its Element. Its representation is a circle, symbolizing an accomplished creation, Time, spirituality, eternity. It has the colour of the full moon. Its seed letter (bij) is HAM, the pure, embracing all speech, it vibrates in the Sushumna. Ether is dressed in white and mounts a white elephant, denoting royal, celestial wealth, peace, knowledge, stability, immutability, the giver of rains and good crops. He symbolizes also the cosmos, 4 pillars supporting a sphere, chastity. At this level the Kundalini moves like an elephant. Akasha is the most subtle element, all pervading; once the Chittakasha (psychic ether) gets purified of all it subconscious movements, stored in the causal body, the yogis become eligible for higher spiritual progress and development.

This plexus is the seat of the Udana Vayu (upgoing vital air) and it is Sattvic by nature.

विशुद्धाख्यंकण्ठे सरसिजममलं धूमधूम्रावभासं
स्वरै सर्वै: शोणैःर्दलपरिलसितैर्दीपितं दीप्तबुद्धेः ।

समास्ते पूर्णेन्दुप्रथिततमनभोमण्ड वृत्तरूपं
हिमछायानगोपरि लसिततनोः शुक्लवर्णाबरस्य ||२८||

भुजैःपाशाभीत्यङ्कुशवरलसितैः शोभिताङ्गस्य तस्य
मनोरङ्के नित्यं निवसति गिरिजाभिन्नदेहो हिमाभः
त्रिनेत्रः पञ्चास्यो ललितदशमुखो व्याघ्रचर्माम्बरढयः
सदापूर्वो देवः शिव इति च समाख्यानसिद्धः प्रसिध्दः ||२९||

Visuddhakhyam kante sarasijamamalam dhumadhumravabhasam
Svaraih sarvaih sonairdalaparilasitairpitam dipta buddheh
Samaste purnendrathitatamanabhomanalah vrttaruoah
Himacchaya nagopari lasitatanoh suklavarnam barasya
Versa 28 sat Chakra Nirupanam

Bhujaih pasabhityankusavaralasitah sobhitangasya tasya
Manoranke nityam nivasati girijabhannadeho himabhah
Trinetrah pancasyo lalitadasmukho vyaghra charmambardhayah
Sadapurvo devah shiv iti cha samakhyansidhi prasidhih
Versa 29 sat Chakra Nirupanam

"in the throat of the lotus called Visuddhi , which is pure and of a smoky purple hue. All the (sixteen) shining vowels on its (sixteen) petals, of a crimson hue, are distinctly visible to him whose 9 Buddhi) is illuminated. In the pericarp of this lotus is the eternal region, circular in shape and white like the full moon. On an elephant white as snow is seated the Bija of Ambhara, which is white of color." Versa 28 sat Chakra Nirupanam

"Of His four arms, two hold the noose and goad, and the other two make the gestures of granting boons and dispelling fear. These add to His beauty. In His lap there ever dwells the great snow – white Deva, three eyed and five faced, with ten beautiful arms and clothed in a tiger's skin." Versa 29 sat Chakra Nirupanam

> सुधासिन्धोः शुद्धा निवसिति कमले शाकिनी पीतवस्त्रा
> शरं चापं पाशं सृणिमपि दधति हस्तपद्मैश्चतुर्भिः
> सुधांशोः संपूर्णः शशपरिरहितं मण्डलं कर्णिकायां
> महामोक्षद्वारं श्रियमभिमतशीलस्य शुद्धेन्द्रियस्य ||३०||

> Sudhasindhoh suddha nivasati kamala sakini pitavastra
> Saram capam pasam srnimapi dadhati hasta – padmis – caturbhih
> Sudhamsoh sampurnam sasapariraitam mandalam karnikayam
> Mahamoksa – dvaram sriyambhimatsilsya suddhendriyasya

"Purer than the ocean of Nectar is the sakti Sakini who dwells in this Lotus. Her raiment is yellow and in Her four lotus hand She carries the bow, the arrow, the noose and the goad. The whole region of the moon without the mark of the hare is in the pericarp of this Lotus. This (region) is the gateway of great Liberation for him who desired the wealth of Yoga and whose senses are pure and controlled."

To put it another way, the Visuddhi is the throat plexus. Ether is the Tattva and Guhya Kali the Mahavidya, SadaShiva and Girija ride a white elephant (sadaShiva is at times called Visnu, which fits well with Garuda, who could be associated in a better manner with the ether element, Akasa) Ham is the Nabho Bija (Ambhara Bija). The beneficent one, Ardhanarisvar, the hermaphrodite, is half Shiva half Sakti, union of the positive and the negative energies. At this level, the intellect has become free from impurities and can sense the Self. SadaShiva is described as five faced and three eyed.

Lalita Dasabhuja, (the ten armed Lalita) holds Tanka, Sula, Krpam (sword), trident, battle axe, Dakhna (fire), Nagenrdra (snake), Ankusa (goad), Pasa (noose) and Abhitikar (or Abhaya Mudra, the signs of no fear). Here, Sakini is the Yogini (but she is Dakini in Sri Vidya). She is the jyoti Svarupa in the form of light with yellow raiment. She is four handed, holding the bow with arrows, the noose and the goad. Dathu is the skin. The endocrines glands are the thyroid responsible for metabolism and parathyroid, the symbol is an azure dot, the sense organs are the ears, speech is the motor organ and sound is the Tanmantra. The color is smoky grey, the Nadi is Sarasvati, the tattva Prana, the Dosa Vata and the Vayu (vital air) Udana meditation on Sakini is light herself, the lunar region, the perfection in Yoga, liberation from diseases and sorrow. The Sadhak becomes the Hamsah that means to say he starts to be really connected with his one's self. Rudra Yamala gives Sakini and SadaShiva Stotram, Kavacha and Sahasranam.

This Chakra has sixteen petals and each vowel of the Sanskrit alphabet adorning each petal.

1	अं	Am Amrtayai Namah
2	आं	Am Akarshinyai Namah
3	इं	Im Indranyai Namah
4	ईं	Im Isanyai Namah
5	उं	Um Umayai Namah
6	ऊं	Um Urdhvakesyai Namah

7	ऋ	Rm Rdidayai Namah
8	ऋम	Rm Rkarayai Namah
9	लम्	Lm Lmkarayai Namah
10	लं	Lm Lmkarayai Namah
11	ए	Em Ekpadayai Namah
12	ऐं	Aim Aisvarayai Namah A is varyatmikayai
13	ओं	Om Omkarayai Namah
14	औम	Aum Ausadayai Namah
15	अं	Am Ambikayai Namah
16	अः	Ah Akasarayai Namah

This Svaras represents the power (Sakti) of the alphabet. They empower all letters, the short ones being Shiva and the long ones Sakti. They are also known as Bija (Shiva) while consonants are known as Sakti. At this level, Mantra becomes "So Ham Hamsah Shivah"

डां सोऽहं हंसश्शिवः

Vishudhi Adishtan Devatayai Dakini Sahit Jiveshwar Svarupinyai Namah

To sum up, Visuddhi Chakra, located at the base of the throat with ruddy filaments, has sixteen petals of smoly purple hue and sixteen red vowels on the petals with Bindu above them. Circular and white, Nabho – mandala is in the pericarp inside which is Candra mandala with elephant – mounted white , garmented and four armed Bija Ham above it, which holds in four hands noose and goad and makes Vara and Abhya Mudras. In his lap is Sada Shiva seated on a great lion - seat placed on the back of the bull. He is in the form of Ardhanarisvar, half the body snow white, Shiva and the other half golden Sakti, with five faces and ten arms holding trident, battle axe, sacrificial sword, thunderbolt, the great snake, bell, goad, noose and making Abhaya Mudra. He wears a tiger's skin, ash all over His body, the garlands of snakes round His neck and down – turned digit of moon on His forehead dropping the nectar. Within the pericarp, in the Lunar region and seated on bones is Sakti Sakini, white in color, four armed, five faced and three eyed on each face, clothed in yellow and carrying in Her hand a bow, an arrow, a noose and a goad.

All these description of the Chakra bears a very esoteric significance linked with spirituality and the inner journey. The presiding Deity is Sadashiva in his form of Ardhanarisvara, joint male-female form, symbol of totality and perfection. He is united inseparably with Girija of white Body.

Shakini is the Shakti presiding over the Tvakdhatu (skin). Shabda (sound) is the tanmatra (rudimentary element). Shortra (sense of hearing) presided by the Dik deveta is the sense of knowledge. Vak (organ of speech) is the organ of action presided by Agni (fire deity). Here sound attains it Vaikhari form, expressed by letters and language. Here we find the principle which increases karmic propensities.

To master this centre 1000 repetitions of the SO HAM HAM SAH mantra are required during 24 hours. Concentration and meditation on this Chakra bring purification of mental attitudes, the attainment of occult powers, knowledge and intense joy. The body gets purified of diseases and impurities. Concentration on this element brings the highest success, total immunity, knowledge of the three periods of time. (Past, present and future).

Related to this Chakra Patanjali Muni writes:

"On the hollow of the throat comes cessation of hunger and thirst." III. 31..

"By conquering the current called Udana Brain the Yogi does not sink in water or in swamps, he can walk on thorns and can die at will." III. 40.

"By making Samyama on the relation between the Akasha and the body and becoming light as cotton wool etc.; through meditation on them the yogi goes through the skies." III. 43 Yoga Sutra.

The Vishuddha Chakra along with the Ajna Chakra play a vital part on the hormonal secretion; it regulates prana (vital force) in the subtle body, the function of the thyroid gland, which operates with other ductless glands, its healthy function being vital at all levels. This centre improves intuition; and protects against occult attacks at different levels. The Thyroid is a very sensitive gland running metabolism.

It is at this throat level that the Jalandhara Bandha should be Practiced, after inhalation. This contraction of the neck helps Prana to unite with the Apana vital air, stops the flow of energy in the Ida and Pingala Nadis. It prevents nectar from (consumption).

Above the Vishuddha Chakra at the root of the palate (Talumula) we find a minor chakra called Lalana Chakra, it is a red lotus having twelve petals representing twelve mental modifications (vrittis):

Sraddha (faith), Santosha (contentment), Aparadha (sense of error), Dama (self-control), Mana (anger), Sneha (affection), Shoka (sorrow, grief), Kheda (dejection), Suddhata (purity), Arati (detachment) Sambhrama (agitation), Urmi (appetite).

(6) THE AJÑA CHAKRA

(Illustration by Swami Jayramdas)

The Ajña Chakra is situated in the space between the two eye brows, known as Trikuti. It corresponds to the cavernous plexus and is situated within the Sushumna Nadi. It is often referred to as the third eye.

It is at the level of the Thalamus the nervous centre which is often known as an unconscious brain seat of instincts, emotions, habits, moods, regulating sleep and the waking state. It directs the whole sympathetic system (neuro. vegetative system). When we receive strong emotional waves, it affects the good function of the body. It also plays a very important part in Yogic practices for concentration. Ajña means "Towards knowledge". It is at this level that the command (ajna) of the Divine Guru from Above is received, to climb to the summits of the thousand petal lotus. This plexus is also known as Mukta Triveni, as the three Nadis Ida, Pingala and Sushumna at this level, go their separate ways.

It corresponds to the Tapar Loka, Abode of the Gods, sphere of Supreme Wisdom, intuition, eternal matter. It rules the Dynamic mental being, will, vision. It is the seat of the inner organ (Anthakarana): Buddhi (intelligence), Chitta (subconscious mind), Ahamkara (the Ego sense with their respective qualities (gunas). Mahat is also the first product of nature (Prakriti) in evolution, it is also known as Cosmic intelligence. But this element is commonly known as Manas Tattva (mental element). The Quality acting at this level is pure Sattva. This Lotus has two petals, of white colour (full moon) on which the two letters HAM and KSHAM are inscribed.

HAM the pure, embracing all speech on the right.

KSHAM the forgiver of sins, the embodiment of illumination on the left. हं हंसवत्यै नमः ।, क्षं क्षमावत्यै नमः ।

Both letters vibrate in the Sushumna.

Between the two petals the Pranava AUM is inscribed in a circle.

The first part of the Pranava stands for the Earth, Fire, the Rigveda, the world Bhur and the deity Brahma (the creator).

U the second part; the intermediate region, the Yajurveda, the Air, the world Bhuva, Vishnu (the maintainer) preserver.

M the third part of the Pranava, the celestial region, the sun, the Samaveda, the world Svar and Maheshvar (the destructor).

A is of yellow colour and unrhythmic (Rajas).

U is rhythmic and white (Sattva).

M is of black colour and of inert quality (Tamas).

The Pranava has eight limbs (Angas): A,U,M,Bindu, Nada, Kala, Kalatita, Tatpara. Four feet: Visva, Taijasa, Prajna and Turya in Vyasti form, macrocosm).

It has three seats: Jagrat (waking), Svapna (dreaming), Sushupti (deep sleep).

Sthula (gross), Sukshma (subtle), Karan (causal) bodies.

Sattva (purity), Rajas (activity), Tamas (inertia).

Kriya Shakti (action), Iccha Shakti (will), Jnana Shakti (knowledge), Past, Present, and Future durations.

Five deities (Brahma, Vishnu, Rudra, Isvara, Sadashiva).

Pranava is the bow, The Atman (mind) is the arrow and the Brahman (godhead) the target. If the aim is accomplished with due care, unity with Brahman is achieved. All the gods take their origin from Omkara; all the three worlds, with every the animate and inanimate therein take their origin from Omkara." (DHYAN BINDU Upanishad)

In this bright or of the Pranava shines the Antar Atma (the inner self) lustrous like a flame and in its light one can see whatever is between the Muladhara and the Sahasrar chakras.

The Presiding deity is Paramashiva (Shambu) in his Hamsa form with his shakti Siddhakali. The white Hakini Shakti with six heads and four arms presides over the Majjadhatu (marrow).

अज्ञानामाऽम्बुजं तद्धिमकरसदृशं ध्यानधामप्रकाशं
हक्षांभ्यां वै कलाभ्यां परिलसितावपुर्नेत्रपत्रं सुशुभ्रम् ।
तन्मध्ये हाकिनी सा शशिसमधवला वक्त्रषटकंदधाना
विद्यांमुद्रां कपालं डमरुजपवटी बिभ्रति शुद्धचित्ता ||३२||

Ajnanamambujam taddhimakarasadrsam dhyana dhama prakasam
Haksabhyam vai kalabhyam parilasitava purnetra patram susubhram
Tanmadhye hakini sa sasisamadhavala vaktrasatkam dadhana
Vidhyam mudram kapalam damarujapavatim bibhrti suddheacitta

"The lotus named Ajna is beautifully white like the moon. On its two petals are the letters Ham and ksam, which are also white and enhance its beauty. It shines with the glory of Dhyana (meditation). Inside it is the Sakti Hakimi, whose six faces are like so many moons. She has also six arms. In one hand she holds book. Two others hands are lifted up in the gestures of dispelling fear and granting boons and with the rest She holds a skull, a small drum and a rosary. Her mind is ever pure (suddha – citta). " Verse 32 Sat Chakra Nirupanam

एतत्पपद्मान्तराले निवसति च मनः सूक्ष्मरूपं प्रसिद्धं
योनौ तत्कर्णिकायामितरशिवपदं लिङ्गचिह्नप्रकाशं
विद्युन्मालाविलासं परमकुलपदं ब्रह्मसूत्रप्रबोधं
वेदनामादिबीजं स्थिरतरहृदयश्चिन्तयेत्तत्क्रमेण ||३३||

Etat padmaantarale nivsati ca manah suksmarupam prasiddham
Yonau tat karanikayamita Shivapadam linga cinah prakasam
Vidyum malavilasam paramkulapadam brahmsutraprabodham
Veda namadi bijam sthiratara hrdayascinta yettat kramena

" Within this lotus dwells the well-known subtle mind (manas). Inside the Yoni in the pericarp is the Shiva called Itara in His Phallic form. Here He shines like a chain of lightning flashes. The first Bija of the Vedas, which is the abode of the most excellent Sakti and which by its luster makes visible the Brahma - sutra, is also here. The Sadhaka with steady mind should meditate upon these according to the prescribed order." Verse 33 Sat Chakra Nirupanam

ध्यानात्मा साधकेन्द्रो भवति पुरपुरे शीघ्रगामी मुनीन्द्रः
सर्वज्ञः सर्वदर्शी सकलहितकरः सर्वशास्त्रार्थवेत्ता
अद्वैताचारवादी विलसति परमापूर्वसिद्धिप्रसिद्धो
दीर्घायुः सोऽपि कर्ता त्रिभुवने संहृतौ पालने च ||३४||

Dhyanatma sadhakendro bhavati parapure sighragami munindrah
Sarvajnah sarvadarsi sakalahitaakarah sarva sastrarthavetta
Advaitacaravadi vilasati parama purvasiddhi prasiddho
Dirghayuh so pi kartta tribhuvana bhavane samhrtau palane ch

"The excellent Sadhak, whose Atma is nothing but a meditation on this Lotus, is able quickly to enter another's body at will and becomes the most excellent among Munis and all - knowing and all - seeing. He becomes the benefactor of all and versed in all the Sastras. He realises his unity with the Brahman and acquires excellent and unknown powers. Full of fame and long - lived, he ever becomes the Creator, destroyer and Preserver of the three worlds." Verse 34 Sat Chakra Nirupanam

तदन्तश्चक्रेऽस्मिन्निवसति सततं शुद्धबुद्धन्तरात्मा
प्रदीपाभज्योतिः प्रणवविरचनारूपवर्णप्रकाशः
तदूर्ध्वेचन्द्रार्द्धस्तदुपरि विलसद् बिन्दुरुपि मकार-
स्तदूर्ध्वे नादोऽसौ बलधवलसुधाधारसन्तानहासी ||३५||

To put it another way, the Ajna Chakra is the two - petalled lotus with Om in the middle. The two letters Ham and Ksam are on the two petals on the sides. It symbolizes the command of the Guru – the Guru comes down (Guru Ajnetir – meaning the descent of the Guru Tattva, the permission or consent given by the Guru to go any further). Paranath is with his white Hakini Sakti. Marrow (Majja Dhatu) is the tissue. Hakini is four armed with Damaru, rosary, skull and Vidya. Om is the Bija, Prana is the Tattva, the sense organ is Manas, the subtle mind, Paramakula Padam, Brahma Sutra Prabodhani Brahma thread is within the Citrini Nadi, which is itself inside the Susmna Nadi.

Itaralingam (Rudra Granthi), the last of the three LIngas, is located inside the Yoni. The Rudra Granthi is the last Granthi (knot) in the upward flow of consciousness. Muladhara knot or Brahma Granthi (symbolized by the black smoky and ill-defined Svayambhu Linga in the heart of the Muladhara Chakra) is the knot in the inconscient linked to sexuality. It represents the material world. Visnu Granthi is the second knot in the way of the Kundalini up to Sahasrar. It is the emotional red (or golden) knot in the heart. It represents the subtle world. Last of three, the Rudra Granthi, black with a very defined outline, is the knot which dissolves the mind into consciousness. These three are very important stages that Sadhakas unfortunately tend to underestimate. It is however necessary to pierce them to allow the fire upward move of the consciousness. The Rudra Yamala gives Hakini and Paranath Mantras and Stotras, Annandsar Mangal Kavach and Paranath Kavach and Hakini and Paranath Sahasranam, which are good for the Sahasrar also, very fine and elevated Sadhanas unknown to the Sadhakas. In the Ardhacandra, the half crescent moon, the mind gets totally detached by Yoni Mudra. It dissolves the action of the Vrittis of the mind.

It is the seat of Manas, the Tanmantra is thought (or Vicara), it is silver white. Nadis are Ida, Pingla and Susumna (it is called Triveni Sangam), the confluence of the three rivers Ganga, Yamuna, Saravati). Prana is the tissue very subtle. Above Ajna are nine centers Indu, Ardhacandra, Bodhini, Nada, Nadanta, Sakti, Vyapika, Samana, and Unmana and finally mahabindu Chakra, each at two fingers from each other. The Citta mind stuff is Khecara about in the sky, ether, devoid of all attachments to worldly things. It becomes minslessness Unmani. We reach now the Abalalaya, the Kamakala triangle with Vama (Rajasic), Jyestha (Sattvic) and Raudri (Tamasic) qualities, an inverted triangle whose three corners are A , Ka and Tha.

आकथादि त्रिरेखाब्जे सहस्रदलमण्डले।
हंसपार्श्वत्रिकोणे च स्मरेत् तन्मध्यगं गुरुं ॥

A – k – tha – di trirekhabhe
Sahasradala mandale
Hamsa parsva trikone ca
Smaret tamadhyagam gurum Verse 58 – Guru Gita

Hamsah is the union of Shiva and sakti. Visarga is the two Bindua at the end of the Hamsah. In this level, the Mantra is Hamsah Shivah SO Ham, So ham Hamsah Shivah (it also works for the Sahasrar). In the endocrine system, the Ajna Chakra corresponds to the pituitary gland which has a role of control over all the other glands. It is related to Uranus (A rsala) (the Sahasrar being linked to Neptune (Varuna))

हां हंसश्शिवस्सोऽहं सोहं हंसश्शिवः

Ajnadhistan devatayai Hakini Sahit paramatma Svarupinyai namah

नादबिन्दुकलातीतं
तस्मै श्रीगुरवे नमः ॥

Nada bindu kalatitam
Tasmai srigurve namah

Makara of Om is the 2 bindus. There is the parabindu placed above the Pranava.Niralambaya tejase, mind`s connection which has no more support into the world has been removed by Khechari Mudra.

इह्स्थानेलीने सुसुखसदने चेतसि पुरं
निरालम्बा बद्ध्वा परमगुरुसेवासुविदिताम् ।
तदभ्यासाद् योगी पवनसुहृदां पश्यति कणान्
तत्स्तन्मध्यान्तः प्रविलसतिरूपानपि सदा ॥३६॥

Iha sthaneline susukhasadane chetasi puam
Niraalambam badhva paramgurusewavasuviditam
Tadabhyaasadu yogi pavansuhradya pashyati kanaam
Tat stnmdhyanth pravilsita rupanapi sada ||36||

"When the Yogi closes the house which hangs without support (the practice of Yoni Mudra) the knowledge whereof he has gained by the service of paramguru and when his Citta by repeated practice becomes dissolved in this place which is the abode of uninterrupted bliss (the Ajna Chakra) he then sees within the middle of and in the space above (the triangle wherein the Pranava is) sparks of fire (or lights) distinctly shinning." verse 36 Sat Chakra Nirupama

It is by the Yoni Mudra that the inner self is restrained and detached from the outside world. The Manas cannot be purified and steadied unless it is completely detached from the material sphere. Therefore, the mind should be completely detached by the practice of this Mudra. Yoni Mudra is thus defined: place left heel against the anus , the right heel on the left foot and sit erect with your body , neck and head in a straight line (siddhas an). Then with your lips resembling a crow`s beak (kaki Mudra) draw in air and fill therewith your belly. Close tightly your ear holes with your thumbs, your eyes with your index fingers, your nostrils by your middle fingers and your mouth by the remaining fingers. Retain the air within you and with the senses thus controlled, meditate on the Mantra until you realize the unity Prana and manas.

We have to make a difference between the Yoni Mudra of Hatha Yoga here described and the Yoni Mudra of the Tantric to salute the deity , both have their value and power but in a different manner.

But it leads to both cases to steadiness of the mind. As by this, the Citta (mind stuff) roams in the ether (kha) by the power of Khechari (spacelessness, Anuttara). Kaki Mudra steadies the mind. The citta is Khechara but when disunited with Manas, devoid of all attachments for worldly things, it becomes Unmani without there is no Yogi. It can be attained by the instructions of the Guru (Guru Kripa Yoga). Susukhasadane is the abode of uninterrupted bliss. Manas with its vritti deprives the Citta from freedom. Disunited from Manas, the Citta moves freely in ether (Khechara) – Unmani state is associated with Khechari Mudra. Again we have to understand that there is the Khechari Mudra and Yoni Mudra of Hatha Yoga, is different Kriya and the khechari Vidya of Sri Vidya which uses a mantra (Khechara). But both are supposed to have the same effect. Nevertheless, The mantra can only work efficiently on an advance Sadhaka. Khechari Mudra practice also is only meant for advanced Hatha yogis who have a capable Guru to guide them in this difficult and dangerous Kriya.

" He sees the light like the clearly shinning morning Sun." it is the region of Fire , Moon and Sun. the inverted triangle (Manipitha) within the A – Ka – tha (Paduka Panchkam) is Abalalayam (Sakti abode). This inverted triangle has three corners representing the Vahni Bindu (A, Fire) at the south, the Candra Bindu (Ka, Moon) at the North East and Surya Bindu (Tha, Sun) at the North West. The triangle formed by the three lines uniting these three Bindus is called Kamakala (Kamakala Rupa), the Abalalaya representing Sabda Brahma. The lines symbolizing will, action and knowledge are called Sakti Vama (from A to Ka, Brahma, Fire, Creation), Sakti Jyesti (from Ka to Tha, Visnu, Moon, Maintenance) and Sakti Raudri (from Tha to

A, Rudra, Sun, Destruction). These Saktis sprout from these three Bindus. The same lines of this triangle are also formed with the fifty – one letters of the Sanskrit alphabet, sixteen vowels from A to Ah, sixteen consonants from ka to Ta and again sixteen consonants from Tha to Sa. the remaining consonants Ha, La and Ksa are located in the inside corners of the triangle. This is the Madhya Trikona of the Sri Yantra, the corollary in the Sahasrar. Gagana is the sky or the empty space above Sankhini Nadi. All things except Atma pass away Parama Shivam, Paranath Hakini.

The Ajna Chakra, or Jnana lotus, is in the region of full moon and it has two petals. Inside it, in the form of Hamsah, is the Bija of Sambhu is in Manidvipa (the island gems of in the ocean of ambrosia) and in its lap is Parama Shiva with Siddhakali on his left – by lap it is meant the space within the Bindus which forms the Visarga at the end of Hamsah. She, the eternal one, stays here in the form of a grain of gram (cana) and she creates beings (Bhutanis). The Bindu should be meditated upon as like this grain of gram consisting of the inseparable couple Shivasaktimayam (Visarga). But the grain refereed to is also divided in two cotyledons under its encircling sheath (Shivasaktisamarasya). It is the region of Pure Candrasaya mandalam, the delightful abode of Visnu. In the center of the ocean of nectar, beyond the countless myriads of world systems, there is the abode supreme of Sri Vidya. Visnu can as well as be called Parama Shiva or SadaShiva. It has been said that Vayu dissolves in Sparsa Tattva and later in Vyoma. So mahanada is the other place of dissolution of Vayu (Vayoh Layasthanam). The place where Vayu ceases to be is called Vayuvini (cf. Rudra Yamala). Prana Sakti ceases when it merges in pure consciousness.

Now is a brief description of an intermediate causal body, the karanaVantara Sarira , a secondary causal service rendered to his Guru , excels in actions in all respects good and by his strong and undivided application in Yoga practices, he then sees the image of Mahanada above Ajna Chakra and becomes perfectly accomplished in speech (Vak Siddhi). Prthvi, the earth, the possessor of rasa, originated from I – Kara, from Ka – kara (which is rasa) the water issued, from Ra – Kara originated fire, from Nada came Vayu which pervades all life and from Bindu originated the Void (Gagana , Akasa, ether) which is empty of all things and which is the sound container. And from all these originated the twenty five Tattvas and finally the universe itself, which is Brahma (fire) and I – Kara which is Mahamaya the Bija Krim is formed. Anusvara or Candrabindu is divided into two, nada which is mahamata (the mother of the universe) and Bindu which is Duhkha – hara, the remover of pain. Sakti herself is thus manifested as Nada Bindu.

ज्वलद्दीपकारं तदनु च नवीनार्कबहुल-
प्रकाशं ज्योतिर्वा गगनधरणी मध्यमिलितम् ।
इह स्थाने साक्षाद् भवति भगवान् न् पूर्णविभवोऽ-
-व्ययः साक्षी वन्हेः शशिमिहिरयोर्मण्डल इव || 37 ||

Jvaladeepankaram tadnu ch navinaarkbahul
Prakashm jyotirva gagandharani madhyamilitam
Iha sthane sakshad bhavti bhagwaan purnvibhvod
Vyayah sakshi vahehe shashi mihir yormmandal iv || 37 ||

" He then also sees the light which is in the form of a flaming lamp. It is lustrous like the clearly shinning morning sun and glows between the Sky and the Earth. It is here that the Bhagwaan manifests Himself in the fullness of His might. " Verse 37 – Sat Chakra Nirupanam

इह स्थाने विष्णोरतुलपरमामोदमधुरे
समारोप्यं प्राणं प्रमुदितमनः प्राणनिधने
परं नित्यं देवं पुरुषजमाद्यं त्रिजगतां
पुराणं योगीन्द्रः प्रविशति च वेदान्तविदितं || 38 ||

Iha sthane vishnortula parama moda madhure
Samaropya pranam pramudita manah prana nidhane
Param nityam devam purusa majamadyam trijagatam
Puranam yogindrah pravisati ca Vedanta viditam || 38 ||

" This is the incomparable and delightful abode of Visnu. The excellent Yogi at the time of death joyfully places his vital breath (his Prana) here and after death enters that supreme, eternal, birthless and primeval Deva, the Purusa, who was before them manifestation of the three worlds and who is known by the vedanta." Verse 38 Sat Chakra Nirupama

To sum up, the Ajna Chakra has two petals and is white. The two Matrkas Ham and Ksam, which are white too, are on the two petals. Hakini, the presiding Sakti of the Chakra, is in the pericarp.

She is white, has six red - colored faces each with three eyes, six arms and is seated on a white lotus. With Her hands She displays Vara - mudra and Abhaya mudra and holds a Rudraksa rosary, a human skull, a small drum and a book. Above Her, within Trikona, is the inner Atma (Antaratma), lustrous like a flame. On its four side floating in the air, are sparks surrounding a light which by its own luster makes visible all between Muladhara and the Brahmarandhra. Above this again is Manas, above Manas is Soma and above Soma in the region of the moon, Kamakala Chakra the Hamsa within whom is Parama Shiva with Sakti. Now that we have studied the Ajna, let us quickly mention the three minor Chakras briefly mentioned in the last sentence above...that is Manas. Soma and Kamakala Chakras. Next to the Ajna be a little higher comes the Manas Chakra , a six petalled lotus corresponding to the sensorium, or the faculties of hearing (Sabda Jnana), touch (Sparsa), sight (Caksus), smell (Gandha), taste (Granapalabdhi) and dream (svapna). This subtle plexus connects the different faculties of the sensorium with each other and with the higher cortex, the nervous system and the body.

Above the plexus, we find the Soma Chakra, a sixteen petalled lotus representing the sixteen Kalas or digits of the moon. It is the seat of the higher mental qualities which are developed by spiritual practices: mercy (Kripa), gentleness (Mrdutva), composure (Dhairya), dispassion (vairagya), constant (Dhrti), prosperity (Sampat), cheerfulness (Hasya), thrill (Romanca), humility (Vinaya), meditation (Dhyan), Quietude (Susthirat), gravity (Ghambhirya), effort (Udyama), non-agitation (Akosbhyam), magnanimity

(Audarya) and one pointedness (Ekagrata).

Still above the Soma Chakra we find the Kamakala Chakra, also called the Niralambapuri (the house or city without support) where the Yogis contemplate the radiant Self and the seven causal bodies (which are lower aspects of the primordial cause , the adya Sakti). This lotus is white with twelve petals located just below the sahasrar Chakra. Twelve Yoga Nadis emanate from this center, represented by the Sanskriti Matrkas : Ham , the pure , embracing all speech , Sam the cause of all , Ksah the embodiment of illumination , the forgiver of sins , Mam the hypnotizer of the opponents , Lam the shinning protector of the world , Vam pure water , Ram fire , Yam the all-pervading sanctifier , Ham , Sam , Kham and Phrem. Om is the seed letter of this Bija which controls the twelve pairs of nerves proceeding from the brain to the sense organs. Like the heart lotus, we meditate on this Chakra as the seat of the Guru.

Now that we have gone through all the other plexuses, we can study the last of them, the sahasrar Chakra (keeping in mind that certain scriptures do not consider it as a real one). Within the pericarp is the yoni on which the Itara Linga stands, shining like lightning (tejomaya); it is the third abode where Maya Shakti (delusion) is very powerful. The Ajna chakra is also the dwelling place of the Rudra Granthi (knot of Rudra). This knot is made by the Antahkarana, specially by the Ego Sense (Ahamkara) which prevents individual consciousness from merging into the indivisible oneness of Divine consciousness. Rudra (the destructor) here destroys the Ego, the root cause of Ignorance; opening the last door, he puts an end to all dualities.

For Mastery of this plexus 1000 repetitions of the SO HAM HAM SAH mantra are required during 24 hours. Concentration and meditation on this plexus destroy all the karmas of past lives, control all adverse circumstances. Liberation while living is achieved (jivan mukti) along with the 8 occult powers and the 32 minor ones. Yogis obtain divine, clear-sightedness.

हां हंसश्शिवस्सोऽहं सोहं हंसश्शि वः ।
आज्ञाधिष्ठानदेवतायै हाकिनीसहितपरमात्मस्वरुपीणयै नमः ।

Ham Hamsahsshiva Ssoham So Hamhamsahsshivah:
Ajnaadhistan devatayai Hakini Sahita
Paramatma Svarupinyai Namah

(7) THE SAHASRAR CHAKRA

(Illustration by Swami Jayramdas)

The Guru Gita says:

"In the round space of the thousand petal Lotus, there is the triangular Lotus which is formed by the three lines beginning with, A,KA,THA and which has HAM and SAH on two sides. One should remember the Guru who is seated in its centre." V.58.

समास्ते तस्यान्तः शशपरिरहितः शुद्धसम्पूर्णचन्द्रः
स्फुरज्ज्योत्स्नाजलः परमरसचयस्निग्धसन्तानहासी
त्रिकोणं तस्यान्तः स्फुरति च सततं विद्युदादाकाररूपं
तदन्तःशून्यं तत्सकल - सुरगणैः सेवितं चातिगुप्तम् ||४१||

Samaste rasyantah sasa parirahitah suddha sampurnacandrah
Sphuraj-jyotsnajalah parama rasacaya snigdha samtanahasi
Trikonam tasyantah sphurati ca satatam vidudakararupam
Tadantah sunyam tatsakala-suraganaih sevitam catiguptam

"within the sahasara is the full Moon without the mark of the hare , resplendent as in a clear sky. It sheds its rays in profusion and it is moist and cool like nectar. Inside the Candra Mandala constantly shining like lightening, is the Triangle and inside it , again shines the Great Void which served by all the Suryas " Verse 41 – Sat Chakra Nirupanam

सुगुप्तं तद् यत्नादतिशय परमामोद सन्तातानराशे
परं कन्दं सूक्ष्मं सकलाशशिकलाशुध्दःरूपप्रकाशं
इह स्थाने देवः परमशिव समाख्या न सिद्धः प्रसिद्धः
स्वरुपी सर्वात्मा रसविरसमितोऽज्ञान मोहान्धहंसः ||४२||

Suguptam tad yatna datisaya paramamoda samtana raseh
Param kandam suksmam sakala sasikalasuddhah prasiddhah
Iha sthane devah paramaShiva samakhya nasiddhah prasiddhah
Svarupi sarvatma rasa virasamito jnana mohandha hamsah

"well concealed and attainable only by great effort is that

subtle Bindu (Sunya) which is the chief root of Liberation and which manifest the pure Nirvana Kala with Ama Kala. Here is the Deva known to all as ParamaShiva. He is the Brahman and the Atma of all beings. In him are united both Rasa and Virasa. He is the Sun that destroys the darkness of all nescience. "Verse 42 - Sat Chakra Nirupanam

Within the white lotus of 12 petals is a triangle which is the counterpart of the Traipura Trikona (yoni) of the Muladhara chakra. It is known as Kamakala. Kama is the creative will. It represents Shiva Shakti. Kala is their manifestation. It represents the Shabdabrahman (Logos) with it's triple aspects and energies. It is the supreme principle (tattva) formed by the three Bindus (dots) : Chandra bindu (lunar), Surya bindu (solar), Vahni bindu (fire), known also as Vimarsha, Prakasha, Mishra bindu. They represent Iccha Shakti, Kriya Shakti' and Jnana Shakti, Brahma, Vishnu, Rudra: Rajas, Sattva and Tamas.

The Lines emanating from the three bindus form the "Hamsah".

The 16 vowels starting from A form the first line: the 16 consonants starting from KA form the second line, the 16 consonants starting from THA form the third line. At the three corners of the triangle, we find the three remaining letters: HA LLA KSHA.

The Hamsah is the root of the mantra. It's body on which the feet of the Guru rest is JNANA MAYA; the wings the AGAMAS and NIGAMAS (Tantric treatises). The two feet SHIVA and SHAKTI; the beak is the PRANAVA (Omkra), the eyes and throat KAMA KALA. The

Hamsah (celestial swan) represents both the masculine and feminine principles, it is immaculate purity. In the region comprised between the Ajna chakra and the Sahasrar is the seat of the causal body (karana sharira) the Seat of bliss (anandmaya kosha) of our soul (jiva). Within that causal body are 7 Shaktis, which are ascending shaktis freeing the Jiva (incarnated soul) from it's Jivahood (bond age). From the Lowest Upwards those Shaktis are known as :

Bindu (ishwara tattva), Bodhini, Nada, Mahanada (sadakhya tattva), Vyapika, Samani (shakti tattva), and Unmani (shiva tattva).We have studied the chakras from the lowest to the highest, but in fact when the Shakti forms the embryo in the mother's womb, it first forms the Sahasrar in the head, the spinal cord latter. It is through the brahmarandhra (fontanelle) that the soul enters the body of the baby after sixth month. It is also through the Brahmarandhra that Yogis separate themselves from their physical body at the time of death, obtaining kapala moksha. The Sahasrar chakra is situated at the crown of the head. The Guru Gita says v 57:

"The Guru's lotus feet, which extinguish the raging fires of mundane existence, are situated in the centre of the white lotus in the region of the moon in Brahmarandhra (the hollow space of the head)."

When the Kundalini reaches this centre, it unites with Lord Shiva and Yogis attain the transcendental conscious state (nirvikalpa samadhi) or supreme bliss (paramaananda).

The Sahasrar chakra possesses a thousand petals of golden blue colour, thousand symbolizes, perfection, infinity, immortality. It's presiding deity is the Paramatma (Godhead) Paramshiva. The all-pervading prana Vayu Vyana (vital air) operates at this level; the quality of the Shakti is sattvic (pure); it is the seat of the Shukra dhatu (semen).

All the previous chakras are found again in a subtler form in the sahasrar. The fifty letters of the Sanskrit alphabet from A to LLA of white colour, go round and round in it's petals twenty times.

SA with Visarga is the seed letter.

ॐ हंसः शिवः सोऽहं

सोऽहं हंसः शिवः

हंसः शिवः सोहं हंसः

हस्ख्फ्रें ह स क्ष म ल व र यूं नमः

Brahma Randhra Sahasradal Sarsij karnikayam yakinim Mamraksaraksa Sukratmanam Sarvanand Chakraya namah

The Sahasrar chakra is the abode of Satya loka or Brahma loka, the abode of supreme bliss and liberation. It rules the higher mind, the illumined mind, and the super mind. It is the abode of Pratibha, the supernatural light, divine light, which grants all knowledge. For mastery of this chakra 1000 repetitions of the SO HAM HAM SAH mantra are required during 24 hours. Meditation on this chakra brings Liberation.

Patanjali Muni writes: "On the light emanating from the top of the head, sight of the siddhas and other divinities is experienced."

According to Shri Aurobindo, the Sahasrar chakra truly speaking is not within the body, it is above the head and it acts as a centre connecting all that is above the mind, extremely subtle with the mind proper situated in the brain. All the movements of the higher mind, intuitive mind, illumined mind and still higher consciousness are first received here and then connected with the mental apparatus. It is the centre of communication between the individual consciousness and the infinite consciousness.

It is the Abode of Parmeshwar and Parameshwari. The Supreme abode of Lalita, so beautifully described by the great poet seer Shri Adya Shankaracharya: "A few blessed ones worship you, the Wave of Bliss and Consciousness, seated on the lap of the supermely Auspicious one, on the couch of auspicious form in the residence of Chintamani, full of Kadamba trees, in the Gem Island surround by Angelic trees amidst the Ambrosial Ocean."

Saundarya Lahari V.8

एतस्या मध्यदेशे विलसति परमपूर्वनिर्वाणशक्तिः
कोट्यादित्यप्रकाशा त्रिभुवनजननी कोटिभागैकरूपा
केशाग्रस्यातिसूक्ष्मा निरवधि विगलत्प्रेमधाराधरा सा
सर्वेषां जीवभूता मुनिमनसि मुदा तत्त्वबोध वहन्ती|| ४८||

Etasya madhyadese vilasati parama purva nirvana saktih
Kotyaditya prakasa tribhuvan janani koti bhagaika rupa
Kesagrasyati suksma niravadhi vigala prema dharadhara sa
Sarvesam jivabhuta muni manasi tattvabhodham vahanti

" within middle space (of the Nirvana Kala) shines Supreme and Primordial Nirvana Sakti. She is lustrous like ten million Suns and is the mother of all three worlds. She is extremely subtle like into the ten millionth part of the end of hair. She contains within her the constantly flowing stream of gladness (prema) and she is the life of all beings. She graciously carries the knowledge of the Truth to the mind of the sages" Verse 48 – Sat Chakra Nirupan

तस्या मध्यान्तराले शिवपदममलं शाश्वतं योगिगम्यं
नित्यानन्दाभिधानं सकलसुखमयं शुद्धबोधस्वरुपम् ।
केचिद् ब्रह्माभिधानंपदमिति सुधियो वैष्णवं तल्लपन्ति
केचिद्धंसाख्यमेततत्किमपि सुकृतिनो मोक्षमात्मप्रबोधम् ||४९||

"within her is the everlasting place called the abode of Shiva , which is free from Maya , attainable only by Yogis and known by the name of Nityananda. She is replete with every form of bliss and is pure knowledge itself. Some call her the Brahman, others the Hamsah. Wise men describe her as the abode of Visnu and rightwous men speak of it as the ineffable place of knowledge of the Atma , or the place of Liberation "Verse 49 – Sat Chakra Nirupanam

Sarvananda maya baindava
Chakre para brahma svarupini
Paramamrut shakti
Sarva mantreshwari
Sarva yantreshwari
Sarva tantreshwari
Sarva vireshwari
Sarva yogeshwari
Mahapurti vidyayai namah

THE BRAIN

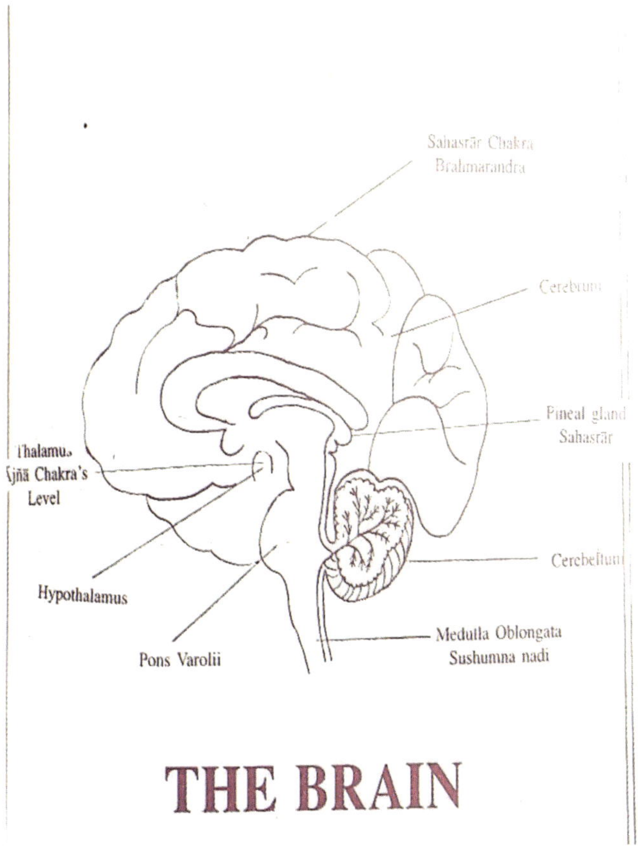

Before studying the different plexuses present in the brain which form the Sahasrar chakra; let us examine briefly their physical counterparts: the cortex the cerebellum, the thalamus, the hypothalamus region, the pons varolii, all playing different functions of our nervous system.

Although the brain represents only 2% of the body's weight, it is the most complex of all our organs, ruling and directing all the functions of our body. Scientist have discovered that the brain contains about 100 milliards of Neurons (nervous cells) which correspond to the number of stars in our galaxy. None of those cells are identical. The brain also needs 50 millilitre of oxygen per minute and the total energy of the cerebral metabolism corresponds to 20 Watts. No less than 30 different chemical components are at work within the brain, some exciting, some inhibiting.

Within the cranium the brain is surrounded by three membranes, the meninges dura mater, pia mater and the arachnoid. Below the arachnoid the brain is surrounded by the cerebro spinal fluid, which protects it against injury. An important system of blood vessels surrounds the brain, bringing incessantly oxygen, 50 millilitre per minute to 100 grammes of brain matter. The cerebrum or Cortex is oval shaped and the larger part of the brain. It can be divided into two halves, the right and left hemispheres separated by a central tissue the "sulcus". Several lobes made up of convolutions "gyrus" divide the cortex into different areas corresponding to different functions. The two hemispheres are not symmetrical in shape and function.

The left hemisphere commands the right part of the body and receives information from the right part of the body. While the right hemisphere commands the left part of the body and gets information's from the left part of the body. Crossing the brain like a semi-circle from one ear to the other, we find two parallel areas in front: The Motor Cortex (commanding movement all over the body) and behind the Somato sensorial area (receiving information from the different parts of the body.)

The area of sight is found at the back of the cortex on the occipital lobe. The area of hearing is situated on the left hemisphere on the temporal lobe just under the start of the motor corex and somato sensorial area. The area of speech is situated on the frontal lobe of the left hemisphere, little above the area of hearing. The area of smell is at the basis of the frontal lobe. At the basis of the temporal and occipital lobe, we find the area of recognizing faces. All these areas relate to each other and work together, but their functions differ in each hemisphere.

Within the cortex we find several other areas which end up the Medulla Oblongata in the Cortex. From the top of the cortex downwards, first comes the Callous body next the Caudal nucleus looking like a tongue, on the top of the Thalamus. The Thalamus is a very vital part of the brain, it is the centre of instincts. Emotions, pain, habits, moods, complexes, unconscious movements. It rules consciousness and sleep. It rules also the whole sympathetic system. It is the controlling point before sensitive messages enter the cortex. It has a constant connection with the cortex, it also regulates temperature in the body.

Just under the Thalamus we find the Hypothalamus and the pituitary gland secreting different hormones, sent to the Thyroid gland, the Adrenals, Subkydney glands and to the testies. These glands control and regulate different function of the body. The Thalamus and Hypothalamus work together, Close to them is the Striatum which influences bodily movements; behind is the Pallidum controlling tonicity. Just under the Pallidum we find the Hypo campus which is the area of memory. Behind the Thalamus we find in the same area the Pineal gland which is regarded as the seat of the soul by Yogis. It plays a prominent part in higher trance states and psychic phenomena.

Just under the cortex at its back, occipital lobe, we find the cerebellum, oblong shaped: it regulates the muscular coordination: the mind rests here during dreams. In front of it, there is the junction where the cerebellum and medulla meet, the Pons Varoli. We have already studied the Ajna chakra controlling the Thalamic and Hypothalamic regions of the Brain. Next to it, a little higher, comes the Manas Chakra, a six petals lotus corresponding to the sensorium or the faculties of hearing touch, sight, smell, taste, and dream (shabda jnana, sparsa jnana, ghranopalabdhi, rasopabhoga and svapna.) This subtle plexus connects the different faculties of the sensorium with each other, the higher cortex, the nervous system and the body.

Above this Chakra we find the Soma chakra, a sixteen petal Louts representing the 16 Kalas of digits of the Moon. It is the seat of Higher mental qualities which are developed by spiritual practices. Krpa (mercy), Mridutva (gentleness), Dhairya (composure), Vairagya (dispassion), Dhriti (constan cy), Sampat (prosperity), Hasya (cheerfuless), Romanca (thrill), Vinaya (humility), Dhyan (meditation), Susthirata (quietude), Gambhirya (gravity), Udyama (effort), Aksobha (non-agitation), Audarya (magnanimity), Ekagrata (one pointedness).

Still above the Soma chakra we find the Kamakala chakra also called the Niralambapuri (the house without support), where the Yogis contemplate the radiant self and the seven causal bodies (lower aspects of the primordial cause, Adhya Shakti). The Lotus is white with twelve petals just below the Sahasara chakra.

12 yoga Nadis emanate from this centre, represented by the Sanskrit letters:

HA the pure embracing all Speech.

SA the cause of all

KSAH The embodiment of illumination forgiver of sins.

MA The hypnotiser of the opponents.

LA the shining protector of the world. VA pure water.

RA fire

YA the all-pervading sanctifier

HA

SA

KHA

PHREM

AUM is the seed letter (bij) of this chakra which controls the twelve pairs of nerves proceeding from the brain to the sense organs. Like the heart Lotus, we meditate on this chakra as the seat of the Guru. Linked to the Paduka Mantra.

(4) THE SEVEN CHAKRAS and THE DUCTLESS GLANDS

Sacchidānanda-rūpāya bindunādāntarātmane |
Adi-madhyāntaśunyāya gurūnāṁ gurave namaḥ||

"To Him who is Being, consciousness and Bliss; who dwells in Bindu and Nada; who has no beginning middle or end; to the Guru of Gurus, be this bow.'

Mahim mūlādharekam api manipüre hutavaham
Sthitam svādhisthāne hrdi marutam ākāśam upari |
Mano'pi bhrūmadhye sakalam api bhittvā kulapatham
Sahasrāre padme saha rahasi patyā viharase ||

(Verse 9 - Saundarya Lahari)

"Having passed through all the tattva centres, earth at the Mooladhar water in Svadhisthan, fire in Manipura, air at the Anahata, Akasa at the Vishuddhi and the mind-tattva in the middle of the eye brows, thou art playing now with thy lord in a secluded place in the Sahasrar."

Sudhādhārāśārais caraṇayugalāntar vigalitaih
Prapañcam Sincanti punar api rasāmnāya mahasā |
Avāpya svām bhūmim bhujaganibham adhyustavalyam
Svamātmānam kṛtvā savapiṣi kulakuṇde kuhariṇi ||

(Verse 10)

"Bedewing the whole of my body with the nectar flowing in continual drops from the feet in Sahasrar and returning to thy own place through the Chandra Nadi, now again dost thou sleep in the hole of Kula Kunda forming thy body like that of a coiled serpent."

This is how Adi Shankara describes the awakening of the Kundalini and its return to the root centre. The language utilized remains very esoteric and succinct. It would be interesting to study and find out the relationship these subtle esoteric chakras have got with the physical apparatus, which remains the frame base of all occult and spiritual undertakings.

To each chakras corresponds a ductless gland also known as endocrine glands playing the role of mediums by which the Kundalini gets her work accomplished within the physical body via the pranamaya kosha. (Vital sheath). Each gland secretes special hormones which are discharged in the blood and circulate through the Nadis of the subtle body. All physical kriyas performed after Shaktipat are only the visible side effects of the discharge of these hormones once certain chakras or glands become more activated.

It is good to note that GURUDEV emphasizes concentration on the AJNA CHAKRA (third eye) at the time of meditation. The gland corresponding to the AJNA CHAKRA is the pituitary gland or hypophysis which is the conductor cell of the whole endocrine system. It secretes a series of hormones called (stimulines) which from a distance, will excite the functions of the thyroid (vishuddhi), pancreas (manipura), adrenal glands (Muladharaa) and gonads [SVADHISHTHAN-MULADHARAA]

In turn when the secretion of thyroid, pancreas, adrenal glands and gonads is sufficient, they will slow down the production of stimulines. The whole of SADHANA is to prepare the physical, vital, mental vehicle for higher descent of DIVINE energy. In this process of inner alchemy, the 7 chakras and their 7 endocrine glands play a major role in inner transformation.

One Sanskrit verse on the KUNDALINI illustrates very well the role of endocrine glands:

'Sarvānandamaya devi Sarva-raksā Svarupini'.

The last part of the verse is significant: the KUNDALINI is the all-giving bliss, the all-protecting goddess. The endocrine glands protect us and they intervene in nearly all processes of self-defence against growth anomalies, weight anomalies, mental anomalies, bone troubles, rheumatic, digestive, nervous and infections troubles, senility etc. Each gland has a peculiar role but all glands are interconnected in a system called general adaptation.

In a normal state each gland have the power to regulate its hormonal outflow as needed: adaptation to cold, heat, toxins aggressions, food, microbes, deprivation, etc. The endocrine system grants this natural self-defence. The cure of all diseases whose origin is to be traced to the anomalies of adaptation can be found in a stable and lasting manner only through a return to hormonal endocrine self-regulation. And this is the first side-effect SHAKTIPAT initiation provides. And now let us study in detail the seven chakras and glands.

The field of activity of these glands is the vital sheath or PRANAMAYA KOSHA, the etheric body whose base is fluids only. The appellation of chakras comes from the etheric vision we can have of their forms, shapes and activity, wheels and lotuses generating viable forms, colours and energies. To follow the verse of SHRI SHANKARA we shall start from the MULADHARA connected with the Adrenals playing a prominent part in the first stages of SADHANA after the Kundalini wakes up.

SHRI AUROBINDO always describes the descent of supreme consciousness above the head, above the thousand petalled lotus downwards. It is a descent of higher consciousness from the abode of Para Shakti, the real meaning of Shaktipat, which leads to an awakening at the base or root of the Muladhara centre. These glands at first play the role of radar or antenna, allowing the descent of higher consciousness into the physical frame and keeping up the relationship with the outer worlds.

THE ADRENAL GLANDS

They have a plane structure and cap the uppermost part of each kidney at the level of the first Lumbar vertebra. They weigh from about 4 to 14 grammes and receive a very rich amount of blood through 60 small arteries. The adrenal glands consist of two parts: the cortico adrenal section, a yellowish, external envelope and the medullo adrenal section, a darker, softer, fragile internal substance.

Both sections are united but have different functions. The cortico-adrenal section is essential for life. It secretes several hormones: aldosterone (hormone of water and salt), cortisol (uplifts glycemia vital to the muscular system), androgen (acts like a sexual mode hormone).

The medullo-adrenal section secretes adrenaline, the hormone of emotion and vigilance that also connects the whole psycho-somatic mechanism. Injection of adrenaline brings about excitement of the sympathetic nervous system, acts upon the circulatory system, the hypertension of arteries, and diminishes the volume of viscera, an effect easily noticeable on spleen and liver.

It also influences upon the breathing system, diminishing the rate of breath, speeding the heart and the respiration, tensing muscles, slightly raising the temperature of the body, increasing the level of glucose in the blood. The general activity of the adrenal glands is increased by emotion, pain, irritation, fear, rage. Hyperstimulation gives great strength, a ruling spirit and greatly increases the sexual expression. Now, all these symptoms of adrenaline action are noted and increased after Shaktipat.

The primary physical KRIYAS, occurring after KUNDALINI wakes up from her sleep at the MULADHARA are the side-effects of a greater activity of the adrenal glands, aiming at strengthening the physical body for further progress. Experiences of fear, increase of the heartbeat and of physical strength, suffocation are all primary Kriyas per formed by the discharge of adrenal hormones. There is a close relationship between the pituitary gland (AJNA CHAKRA) and the adrenal glands as they have a co-operative effect on the brain and on the sexual cells.

Correct balance of the adrenal glands is achieved through the full activity of the pituitary gland. The adrenal glands are the glands of fight. Ruled by Jupiter they give great strength, optimism and induce a ruling spirit. They are closely related to the brain.

Brain fatigue is often due to adrenal fatigue. The adrenal glands are also connected to the sexual glands and to the pancreas [MANIPURA CHAKRA). It is through the secretion of iodine by the thyroid glands that the adrenal glands receive their potential energies. The MULADHARAA CHAKRA is therefore very important. It is the basic pole of the KUNDALINI, the MULA TRIKONA, base triangle, where the triple SHAKTI lies dormant. A well-balanced function of the adrenal glands is vital for further spiritual development.

The adrenal cortex contains more phosphorus-bearing sub stance. It has a close relation with the grey matter of the brain, also with sex and the chemical contents of blood, correlated to the voluntary nervous system. The secretion of the cortex is called internalin, which stimulates a healthy growth of the brain and of the sex-cells. It also develops great mental concentration and physical endurance. It generates a vigorous nervous and muscular constitution; Cortisol affects the metabolism of protein into glucose. Aldosterone affects the body's ability to retain sodium. The inner section of the adrenal glands contains numerous nerve-cells belonging to the sympathetic nervous system.

The adrenal glands eliminate waste from the blood, induce a re-enforcement of the nutritive properties of the blood, tone the muscles, improve the activity of the brain, of the sympathetic nervous system. It assimilates the proteins connected with the spleen, thymus and thyroid gland.

The action of adrenalin is regulated by the sympathetic or involuntary nervous system. Deficiency brings weakness, sensitiveness to cold, cold hands and feet, loss of appetite, mental instability, a tendency to worry and thoughts of suicide. Therefore, a good functioning of the adrenal glands is essential. Once the KUNDALINI is awakened by Shaktipat her prime work is to remove every kind of misfunctioning or imbalance.

THE GONADS

[SVADHISTHANA CHAKRA]

From the Greek word gonos or seed.

In women: ovaries, uterus, vagina, breast glands.

In men: testicles, spermatic duct, penis, prostate gland.

The SVADHISTHANA CHAKRA is connected to the reproduction glands (gonads) which regulate the production of sperm and ova, development of secondary sexual characteristics such as growth of hair, voice, menstruation, development of breasts.

The ovaries are governed by the Moon, the testicles are governed by Mars.

The male gonad is the testicle where spermatozoids are formed and stored up in the prostate glands. The latter has a very important influence on personality and character. The testicle has a double function: endocrine and exocrine. The endocrine function is to make the testerone act on muscular and skeleton development while giving vitality to the brain, this latter function being under the control of the hypophysis.

The exocrine function is the making of spermatozoids. Once the KUNDALINI traverses the SVADHISTHANA CHAKRA, heat is generated and an increase in sexual urge is experienced. The sacral centre relates to the throat centre (VISUDDHA) and the energies of the sacral centre must be re-directed towards the throat. The process is called URDHVARETA or sex sublimation. This sexual energy, utilized for spiritual upliftment, has a tremendous power but it is only through Guru's grace that this transformation/sublimation can be achieved successfully.

THE PANCREAS

[Solar plexus - MANIPURA CHAKRA]

The pancreas corresponds to the solar plexus [MANIPURA CHAKRA] located behind the stomach. It is governed by the cancer sign and Mars. It is a gland of both internal and external secretion. It is oblong from right to left and has the form of a hook. The cells of the pancreas secrete insulin, which helps the entry of glucose into the cells and its consumption by the cells acting on the liver's ability to store and utilize sugar.

The cells of the pancreas secrete glucagon whose complex action furthers the use of glucose. The pancreas corresponds to the solar plexus, MANIPURA, which influences upon the activity of the stomach, of the liver, of the gall-bladder and of the nervous system.

It is at this level that the cause of all psychosomatic diseases is to be found. Digestion is governed by the MANIPURA CHAKRA, the home of PRANA (vital force), situated behind the navel and concerned with the fire of the body, which is used in digestion and the metabolism of food. It also coordinates the nerves of the stomach, intestines, and other abdominal organs. The digestive fire depends on a supply of PRANA from MANIPURA. It burns up all the toxins of the body and eliminates indigestion. NAULI KRIYA and UDDHYANA BANDHA are often performed automatically after SHAKTIPAT to allow the MANIPURA CHAKRA to function in a better manner.

THE SPLEEN

The vital energy of the SUN [PRANA) is assimilated by the etheric centre of the spleen.

The spleen channels vitality throughout the body. The sacral centre is the spiritual counterpart of the spleen. It is in the spleen that the negative energy of matter encounters the positive energy, Prana. There is a panic relationship between the spleen centre and the coronal centre. The spleen protects against the intrusion of diseases, vitalizes the blood and purifies it.

It is a lymphoid organ containing red and white cells and it destroys the old red blood cells. It is located at the left end of the stomach, between the latter and the diaphragm. It is bean shaped and has a deep bluish colour. It is soft, spongy, and fragile. The spleen always enlarges during digestion. This gland is fed by the splenic artery and its veins empty into the portal vein which discharges its contents into the liver. The secretion of the spleen is called haemolytic and is the controller of the blood destruction.

The spleen manufactures white blood corpuscles, stores iron and has a strong influence on the nervous system. It controls the intake of vital sugar fluid which traverses the **ner**ves. It helps to the digestion through the vital essence received from the SUN. The spleen is the entrance gate for the solar force which vitalizes the dense body. From the spleen this sun force is sent to the solar plexus where it meets the ether which has been extracted from the blood in the heart.

It flows along the silver cord to the solar plexus where the seed atom of the vital body is located. The fluid has a light pink colour. It flows along the filaments composing the nervous system and permeates every part of the physical body energizing each and every cell with its life force. In healthy persons this life energy radiates outwardly through the pores of the skin. It drives out poisonous gases and dangerous microbes. It protects against diseases.

The spleen is associated with the etheric region, It is ruled by the sun, will, vitality, authority. It vibrates to golden yellow. It opens into the entire etheric region. The practice of SURYA NAMASKAR and recitation of GAYATRI have a very good strengthening effect on the spleen.

THE THYMUS

(ANAHATA CHAKRA]

The thymus is related to VENUS. It is concerned with the creation of antibodies and acts as a defence against bacteria, viruses and foreign invaders. The secretion of the thymus is called thymidine believed to be the controller of child growth.

The thymus also acts as a storage and reserve organ granting protection and controlling normal bone growth and muscular metabolism. It influences upon the development of the adrenal cortex, of the pineal gland, of the prostate gland and of the thyroid. It is situated in the lower part of the neck in front of the wind-pipe. It is a white rosy coloured soft organ. It has two lobes. The thymus is mostly related to all life and blood. It is the centre which attracts the silver cord of the soul to enter its body. It is closely related with the pineal gland and sexual functions.

The normal activity of the thymus is to regularize the sympathetic nervous system, as well as blood and the vagus nerve. It is through the vagus nerve that the energies entering through the coronal centre are distributed to the rest of the body. The vagus nerve starts from the bulb, goes down the neck along the carotids, passes through the thorax and ends in the abdomen.

Two centres are connected to the vagus nerve: the MULADHARA and the ANAHATA CHAKRAS when the SAHASRAR, ANAHATA and MULADHARA are in a dynamic and magnetic relationship they create a lightning effect acting on the vagus nerve. At the time of leaving the body the seed atom of the heart rises through the vagus nerve and leaves the body by the BRAHMA RANDRA.

THE THYROID

[VISHUDDHA CHAKRA]

The word thyroid is derived from the Greek word "thuroeides' which means "having the form of a shield". It is the biggest of all the endocrine glands. It is situated in the region of the neck in front of the wind-pipe. It weighs from 25 to 30 grams. The tissues of the thyroid have the same origin as those of the ant-hypophysis. It secures the balance of all the different components of the physical body. It relates to SHAKTI, the vowels of the alphabet, the HOLY GHOST. It has a fundamental effect on the psyche, mental being and body.

It is ruled by MERCURY's planetary spirit and manifests itself essentially as reason, intellect, good memory, eloquence, dexterity, self-expression, self-mastery. It is related to the LORD of MIND, the goddess of speech. It keeps up a balance of power between the organs of generation and the brain. It rules the lower self and produces spiritual growth. It vibrates to the colour purple. The thyroid controls the rate of metabolism, especially the speed at which the ingested food is burnt in the body.

It regulates body heat, growth and development. The importance of the thyroid is clearly indicated by the richness of its circulation. It receives about 4 times as much blood, in proportion to its size, as do the kidneys. Its secretion is called thyroxin, a gelatinous substance containing a large percentage of iodine. It also contains arsenic and phosphorus. Thyroxin depends on iodine for its activity.

The thyroid is an energy gland and its secretion controls the speed of living. The corresponding subtle CHAKRA is the VISUDDHA CHAKRA whose Sanskrit letters are the vowels, embodying SHAKTI power. The thyroid is the most important gland in the body because it controls the growth of the dense vehicle and mental development, closely related to all the other six glands. It is the great link between the brain and the organs of generation and manufactures the secretion necessary to maintain brain balance.

It acts on the skin, the skin glands, hair, mucous, membranes, irritability, response of the nerves. The thyroid raises the energy level of the brain and the whole nervous system. The spiritual solar life essence contained in the thyroxin gives balance to the brain and life to the organs of reproduction. The thyroid maintains in the blood the same amount of iodine as there is in the sea: one litre of iodine per 100 litres of blood. The thyroid acts specifically on the growth of the internal and external tissues of the body, on the growth of nerves and brain tissues.

The hormones of the thyroid act on the heart rhythm and

blood flow, the nervous system, the muscles, the skin, the regulation of temperature in the body, on the resistance to all outer aggressions: The level of iodine in the body is responsible for a good functioning of the thyroid. The thyroid is the organ of emotion. The adrenal glands derive their power from the thyroid iron.

THE PARATHYROID GLANDS

They are concerned with the metabolism of calcium and phosphorus, necessary for the development of strong and healthy bones. The parathyroid glands are four small. glands of the size of a lentil behind the thyroid. The parathormone elevates the amount of calcium in the blood, controls the metabolism of calcium or calcareous salts in the organism, which is essential for the balance of the nervous system and the control of muscles. The parathyroid glands are closely associated with the pituitary glands and must maintain harmony with the cosmic forces.

Because of their action the aura of man is harmonized with the spiritual vibrations of the soul and a balance is established between the cerebro-spinal system and the sympathetic system. The pituitary gland is closely associated with the thyroid and parathyroid glands.

THE PITUITARY GLAND OR HYPOPHYSIS

(AJNA CHAKRA)

When reached, this CHAKRA reveals the AJNA or the commands of the great GURU seated on the SAHASRAR PADMA. The eyebrow centre relates to the pituitary gland, the master gland of the body as it regulates the functioning of the other glands, stimulating or inhibiting their secretions according to the body's requirements.

The hypophysis or pituitary glands has the size of a pea and weighs about 0.5 grams. It plays a vital role, by its hormones, through its action on the other glands and its relationship with the two nervous systems, cerebro-spinal and sympathetic. It is situated at the base of the brain under the floor of the third ventricle close to the optic chiasma, at its higher level, from which it is separated by a small membrane. It secretes several hormones which stimulate the secretion of the other endocrine glands.

It is the maestro of the endocrine glands and is itself directed by the nervous system. The pituitary gland is often referred to as the somatic brain as it is the centre of subconscious actions. The gland consists of two parts, an anterior lobe, with a positive polarity and a posterior lobe with a negative polarity. The anterior lobe or ante-hypophysis is the keystone of the endocrine system.

This lobe assimilates the vital energy stored in the oxygen which we breathe, re-distributing it to the brain, to the cerebrospinal system, to the psychic or sympathetic system. The cell elements of the anterior lobe show 7 types corresponding to the 7 hormones secreted by the outer hypophysis. The lobe also exerts great power over the sexual force and creation. The pituitary gland also exerts an influence over the human skeleton.

The anterior lobe is responsible for the mental and intellectual capacities while the posterior lobe rules over feelings and emotions. A man with a strong personality and well-balanced has the two lobes of the pituitary gland in good working order. The removal of the pituitary glands brings about total physical ruin. This gland keeps up a harmonious relationship between physical and spiritual forces and furthers their mutual interaction in order to regenerate all cells and tissues and to maintain a fair balance. The pituitary gland keeps up the same percentage of salt as is to be found in the sea.

The right eye is the medium of desire forces and emotion. The left eye conveys concrete mental forces. The third eye is the result of the vibratory interaction between the forces of the soul acting via the pineal gland and the forces of personality, of the ego, acting through the pituitary gland. These positive and negative forces bring light on the head. The pituitary gland produces no less than eight different hormones. The anterior lobe of the pituitary gland called the pre pituitary is composed of a collection of solid columns of cells surrounded by blood spaces into which the cell secretion is undoubtedly directly poured.

The posterior lobe consists of secretory cells producing a glossy substance which finds its way into the spinal fluid that bathes the nervous system. This gland is situated in a saddle-shaped depression of the sphenoid bone between the eyes and directly behind the roof of the nose and at the junction of the two optic nerves. It is the central station through which all growth is directed. It is smaller in man than in woman. The anterior lobe exerts control over the body structure of the skeleton. The posterior lobe rules over the circulation of fluids in the body. The pituitary gland is connected directly with and rules over the outer sheath of the brain and spinal column, the dura mater.

This sheath embodies the great protective mother principle. It covers the brain and spinal cord protecting them against outer impacts and also feeding the blood vessels and nerves. There is a chemical substance in the secretion of the pre pituitary gland that stimulates the growth of tissue, bony tissue and another tissue that influences upon sex organs and sexual activity, stimulates well-being and action of the thyroid and adrenal glands.

The internal secretions of the pituitary gland influence the energy production, especially on the energy of the central nervous system, on grey matter and the spinal cord. The pituitary gland receives an abundant blood supply. An active pituitary gland produces alertness, a dull pituitary gland produces sleepiness. So, we can understand why it is so important to concentrate on that spot during meditation to allow a better work of the gland and of the whole chakra system. Very often in yogic treatises reference is made of drops of nectar coming from different centres of the brain, supposed to rejuvenate the body, free it from hunger, thirst etc. This nectar is no other than the different secretions of hormones emerging from the pineal and pituitary glands.

Meditation, the recitation of different mantras with appropriate concentration and mudras, asanas, play a very important role in the good functioning of these glands. The glands have still a higher level of vibration and functions which can be directed towards curing diseases, granting psychic powers and higher spiritual development the effects differing with the use of different MANTRAS. Therefore, this mantric science must be used in a very cautious manner to avoid a misfunctioning of the glands. The pituitary secretion stimulates the brain cells direct ly naturally. It assists in energy transformation, expansion and conversion, particularly of the brain and sexual systems.

It works with the creative force both in the brain and in the reproduction organs. The pituitary gland is a male/female gland. The female type is dominated by the post pituitary lobe of the gland (emotions and refined sentiments). The male type is dominated by the anterior lobe (power to control, high brain power, ability to learn). The anterior lobe is called the gland of intellectuality and of the capacity of the mind to control its environment. This dual male/female aspect of the gland brings to mind the esoteric worship of the GURU'S SANDALS (PADUKA), symbol of SHIVA and SHAKTI.

The pituitary glands act more on the framework of the body, skeleton, mechanical supports and motions. It stimulates the brain cells more directly. The pituitary gland facilitates energy consumption. It is under the rule of Uranus, responsible for originality, universality, love, liberty, compassion, ingenuity, independence, reformation, intuition, clairvoyance, mysticism, altruism and super consciousness. It vibrates to yellow light.

The Fivefold Footstool (Paduka Panchakam)

I meditate on the Guru in the Lotus of a thousand petals, which is radiant like the cool rays of the full moon and whose lotus hands makes the gestures which grant blessings and dispel fear. His raiment, garland and perfumes are ever fresh and pure. His countenance is benign. He is in the Hamsah in the head. He is Hamsah Himself.

ब्रहमरन्ध्रः सरसीरुहोदरे नित्यलग्नवदातमद्भुतम्

कुण्डलीविवरकाण्डमण्डितंद्वादशार्णसरसीरुहं भजे ॥

Brahmarandhra sarsiruhodare
Nitya lagna mavadata madbhutam
Kundali vivarakanda manditam
Dvadasar nasara siruham bhaje

I adore the wonderful white lotus of twelve letters, which is within the womb of and inseparable from the pericarp of the lotus in which is the brahmrandhra and which is adorned by the channel of kundali. (paduka Pancakam – verse 1)

तस्य कन्दलितकर्णिकापुटेक्लृप्तरेखमकथादिरेखया

कोणलक्षितहलक्षमण्डली भावलक्ष्यमबलालयं भजे ॥

Tasya kandalita karnikapute
Klpta rekha maka thadirekhaya
Kona laksitahakasa mandala
Bhava laksyamabala layam bhaje

I adore the abode of Sakti in the place where the two pericarps come together. It is formed by the lines A, Ka, Tha and the letters Ha, La, Ksa which are visible in each of its corners and which give it the character of the Mandala. (paduka Pancakam – verse 2)

तत्पुटे पटुतडित्कडारिमस्पर्धमानमणिपाटलप्रभम्

चिन्तयामि हृदि चिन्मयं वपुर्नादबिन्दुमणिपीठमण्डलम् ॥

Tatpute patuna ditka darima
Sparddha manamani patala prabham
Cintayami hrdi cinmayam vapor
Nadabindu manipitha manadalam

In my heart I meditate on the jeweled altar (manipitha) and on Nada and Bindu as within the triangle forespoken. The pale red glory of the gems in this altar shames the brilliance of the lightening flash. Its substance is Cit. (paduka Pancakam – verse 3)

उर्द्ध्वमस्यहुतभुक्शिखात्रयं तद्विलासपरिवृंहणास्पदम्

विश्वघस्मरमहोच्चिदोत्कटं व्यामृशामि युगमादिहंसयोः ॥

Urdhavamasya huta bhukasikha trayam
Tad vilas apari brahanas padam
Visvaghasmara mahoc – cidot katam
Vyamrsami yuga madihamasyoh

I intently meditate on the three lines above it (Manipitha) beginning with the line of fire and on the brilliance of Manipitha which is heightened by the luster of those lines. I also meditate on the primordial Hamsah which is the all-powerful great light in which the universe is absorbed. (paduka Pancakam – verse 4)

तत्रनाथचरणारविन्दयोःकुङ्कुमासवपरिमन्दयोः।

द्वन्द्वमिन्दुमकरन्दशीतलं मानसं स्मरति मङ्गलास्पदं ॥

Tatra nathacarana ravindayoh
Kumkumasava parimarandayoh
Dvandvam indu makaran dasitalam
Manasam smarati mangalaspadam

The mind that contemplates the two lotus which are the feet of the Guru and of which the ruby – colored nectar is the honey. These two feet are cool like the nectar of the moon and are the place all auspiciousness. (paduka Pancakam – verse 5)

निसक्तमणिपादुकानियमिताघकोलाहलंस्फुरत्किसलयारुणंनखसमुल्लसच्चन्द्रकम् ।

परामृतसरोवरोदितसरोजसद्रोचिपं भजामि शिरसि स्थितं गुरुपदारविन्दद्वयम् ॥

Nisaktamani paduka niyamitagha kolahalam
Sphurat kisa layarunam nakhasam ullasaccadrakam
Paramrta sarovarodita sarojasa drocisam

Bhajami sirasi sthitam gurupada ravind - dvayam

I adore in my head the two lotus feet of the Guru. The jeweled footstool on which they rest removes all sin. They are red like young leaves. Their nails resemble the Moon shinning in all Her glory. There is the beautiful luster of lotuses frowning in a lake of nectar. (paduka Pancakam – verse 6)

पादुकापञ्चकस्तोत्रं पञ्चवक्त्रादिनिर्गतं

षडाम्नाय फ़लप्राप्तं प्रपञ्चे चातिदुर्लभं

Paduka pancana stotram panca vaktra dvinirgatam
Sadamnaya phala praptam prapance catidurlabham

This hymn of praise of the fivefold footstool was uttered by Him of five faces. By the recitation and hearing of it is attained that good which is gained by the recitation and hearing of all the rhymes in praise of Shiva. Such fruit is only attainable by great labor in this wandering Samsara. This Paduka Pancakam has great esoteric meaning and power, always used by Vidyaists. It is different from the one given before the Guru Gita but both expose the greatness of Guru`s feet, the essence of all practices.

THE PINEAL GLAND OR EPIPHYSIS [SAHASRAR CHAKRA]

SHRI AUROBINDO refers to the SAHASRAR CHAKRA as the centre of supramental consciousness, even above the head, above the thousand petalled lotus. It is the abode of the PARA SHAKTI, the highest point up to which individual consciousness can be retained. It typifies the spiritual plane and is the permanent abode, the goal to which we must lead the Kundalini, the place where all our energies should be directed.

BINDU IS SHIVA, RAJAS IS SHAKTI THE MOON IS BINDU, RAJAS IS THE SUN

It is at the SAHASRAR that the supreme BINDU emanates from the union of KUNDALINI with SHIVA. This divine union is known to the highest ascetics when the union of the two is affected. It is called PARABRAHMA where It is only one without a second. Within the TRIKONA (triangle at the MULADHARA) is RAJAS.

Within the TRIKONA of SAHASRAR is SHUKLA.

When these two negative and positive forces meet divine sight is achieved.

"Thou art playing now with thy LORD in a secluded place in the SAHASRAR."

The pineal gland is a tiny gland in the brain weighing only 0.16 grams. It looks like the fruit of the pine-tree and is situated at the centre of the brain in a small cavity behind and above the pituitary gland. It plays an important part in the psychology of behaviour. It has a vital function as a connecting link between the different levels of awareness above and behind the physical plane. Through the stimulation of this gland, one is able to contact the deeper layers of the mind awareness, intuition, visualisation and imagination.

It is a cone-shaped, reddish body, half an inch in length, the size of a grain of wheat and attached to the roof of the third ventricle of the brain. It is composed partly of nerve cells containing a pigment like the cells of the retina. It is he centre of divine and spiritual vision. In children this centre is very active as they work on intuition and spontaneous awareness. The pineal gland atrophies from the age of 8 owing to the activity of the five senses and objective consciousness. The pineal gland is supposed to transfer the impressions of the subjective world to the psychic being.

It is the transformer and connecting rod which transfers the intelligence of psychic consciousness to objective consciousness. It is within the pineal gland that contact with the over soul is achieved. The secretion of the gland called pineal in acts as an inhibitor for all the glands of internal secretion. It also acts as a general supervisor of all the other glands. It secretes 3 hormones:

1-Melatonin formed from serotonin with the help of an enzyme of the epiphysis cells. The activity of the enzyme is related to the light giving of the retina. The pineal gland enriches itself with serotonin during day time and with melatonin at night.

2-Glomerulotropin which influences upon and controls the secretion of aldosterone through the cortical adrenal glands. There is a relationship between the pineal gland and the function of the thyroid. Along with the adrenal glands the pineal gland acts upon the pigmentation of the skin. It is also connected with the sexual glands and the brain.

Melatonin, the secretion of which varies with light, is believed to be basis of the human biological clock. Melatonin inhibits the sexual and thyroid functions and affects brain activity. The pineal gland receives a rich blood supply which stimulates its activity. It controls the action of light on the pigmentation of the skin. It causes the normal physical and mental development of the brain cells and the normal development of the cells of the reproduction organs.

The pineal gland becomes calcified and buried in lime salts and becomes weak and the muscles do not receive the proper amount of nourishment.

The practice of SURYA NAMASKAR, combined with certain pranayama's, mudras and recitation of the GAYATRI MANTRA can slow down the decay of the pineal gland. These practices seek to maintain a good functioning of the gland, uplift and control the human character. The pineal gland is ruled by NEPTUNE, the light-bearer for the spiritual sun.

This planet is per excellence occult, prophetic and spiritual It raises man above the human weaknesses and makes him divine. It results in knowledge above reason, spirituality, inspiration, clairvoyance, prophecy, devotion, ability to contact the celestial occult realms. When aroused it lifts consciousness to the world of the divine spirit and to true knowledge of God. And, then the seeker gets knowledge of the other solar systems, gods, etc.

The pineal gland vibrates to beautifully dazzling blue and is closely associated with initiation. The activity of the pineal gland greatly helps in control ling the mind. Its size varies according to the mental and spiritual status of the person. It is also connected with the functions of the interstitial part of the brain. The pineal gland is held in place by the diameter, a membrane that envelops the brain and the spinal cord from which the entire central nervous system is fed.

The diameter is the innermost sheath. The pineal gland is the male, positive organ, the abode of lord Shiva. "The TRUTH POWER" is not confined to that centre alone; from there it externalizes and pervades the whole system, infuses itself in all the centres known and unknown of the SUPERMIND", says AUROBINDO

All this inner subtle chemistry of the endocrine system, is highly enhanced by the Alchemy of the several mantras, mudras and meditation of Sri Vidya of the kundalini Sakti.

GODDESS KUNDALINI, THE MOTHER OF YOGAS

"He bearing in his hand all manly might, shuts himself up in deep Hollows (of the inner cavity of hearing the heart.

But he delegates his strength to the true seekers.

When these sages pray with heart felt devotion they realize this divine fire through deep meditation. "Rigveda 1. 67.2.

"He himself, eternal and unborn, holds the broad earth up; . and with his Divine will sustains the sky.

Oh Fire Divine, verily you are the life force of even the remotest corners hidden in deep caves." Rigveda 1.67.3

"Whosoever knows the inner fire, hidden in far off places, who constantly submit, to the Holy Law and who adores him, with sacred hymns, truly God blesses them with true guidance to attain wealth." Rigveda 1.67.4

Although variously named and described, the Kundalini stands at the root of all spiritual practices. She is the key, opening the doors of the soul's evolution, the essence of self-realization and Liberation. No adequate words can describe Her glories, which are as infinite as Infinity. From time immemorial, Yogis and Seers have known her, and discovered through introspection the various techniques and means to awaken her and allow her to transform the base metal into Pure gold Divine. She is the Divine force who remodels the Pashu (lower man) into the Divya (divine) man, she is the essence of all Yoga's, Tantras and other scriptures that have survived to the up levels of time and ages. Although in recent time, many people have come to know about her existence, her secrets remain the property of the few high initiates who continue to unfold and maintain the unbroken line of Gurus.

"To be worshipped by those turned inwards, she is difficult of access to the extroverts." Lalita Sahasranam. Antar Mukha

The late, world recognized Paramhans Yoganandji declared that her yoga was an instrument through which human evolution could be quickened. He had found that in three years of intelligent practice a yogi was able to obtain the same result that Nature takes a million years to achieve, Lord Shiva (Lord of Yogis) tells his Divine consort Parvati in the Guru Gita: "O Beautiful One, they are liberated in Pinda, whose Kundalini is awake."

They are liberated in Pada who hear spontaneous repetition of the HAM SAH. They are liberated in Rupa who have envisioned the blue point (Nila Bindu). But they are undoubtedly liberated who experience the Transcendental state beyond form in Rupatita." V.122.

The Yogasikhopanishad says:

"There is Liberation for one having a sight of the Middle Nadi (the Sushumna abode of the Kundalini). One discoursing on the Sushumna is rid of all sins and will attain eternal bliss. The Sushumna alone is the holiest place of pilgrimage. The Sushumna alone is Meditation of the Highest order. The Sushumna alone is the Worthiest Goal." V.41-46.

"This path of the Higher Kundalini conquers the Macrocosm". Kundalini Upanishad. III 43.

The aim of all the various kundalini practices is Liberation, freedom from physical, mental, emotional karmic bondage; awareness of the undivided Divine consciousness.

Guru Vasishta thus imparts this Knowledge to Lord Rama:

"Kundalini functions in the body composed of the fivefold elements in the form of life force. It is the same Kundalini which is known variously as conditioning or limitation, as the mind, jiva, movement of thought, intellect determining faculty, ego sense, for it is the supreme life force in the body. It is the supreme power in all beings and it is the prime mover of all power. It is when the Kundalini unfolds and begins to move that there is awareness within oneself. Hence the Kundalini is the very seed of consciousness, understanding and knowledge.

When the light of consciousness is seen the darkness of Ignorance and the cycle of becoming comes to an end. "Yoga

Vasishta, Nirvana Prakaranam, VI.1. 4294.. At the time of Death of the physical body, the Soul and the Astral body leave their mortal frame by any of its nine apertures, which correspond to different levels of evolution, after visualizing past karmas of several life times along with future ones. As it is said in the Bhagavad Gita the last thought at the time of death will determine the future rebirth.

The Soul will now transmigrate in the astral body and spend a certain time in different realms, corresponding to its evolution before re-entering a new womb. Human birth is essential and a blessing for further spiritual evolution. The new body of the baby in the womb, its sex, his parents his social and human surroundings, the place and date of birth are all factors fitting with the past karmas and future ones to be worked out by the departed soul now seeking rebirth.

It is only in the seventh month, when the baby's body has taken a definite shape that the soul along with its astral body will enter their new body through the fontanelle, the astral fluid, linking the astral body with the new physical one. The different parts of the Astral and Causal bodies responsible for this new incarnation will fit to their physical counterparts, along the spine in the different chakras, storehouses of the features of the character of the future born child.

The Cosmic Kundalini after creating the child's body now assumes an individual form following the evolutionary course of the incarnated soul and gets coiled up at the base of the spine in the lowest chakra called Mooladhar. She will remain there dormant till time, good Karmas the grace of God and enlightened beings awake her and allow her to move upwards, opening new realms of spiritual unfoldment.

"He who fell from Yoga is reborn in a house of the pure and wealthy or in the family of wise Yogis; There he comes into contact with knowledge acquired in his former body and strives more than before for perfection. "Bh. Gita VI. 41-43.

All the scriptures are unanimous to declare that the human body is the highest one can obtain in the whole of creation. It is the medium best fitted for spiritual practices and attainment of perfection. Even the gods seeking spiritual emancipation must incarnate themselves as human beings. The Microcosm dwelling in the human body truly resembles the Macrocosm of the Universe. The Individual Kundalini is the exact replica of the Cosmic Mother Goddess.

But until and unless we become aware of them, this physical body is only the cause of bondage, Yoga is to transform this physical frame that undergoes all kinds of experiences into a perfected medium able to receive and control the means and energize leading to eternal perfection. Of course, this task is very hard, dangerous, and complex, but it is indeed the very aim of life.

Shri Shankaracharya says:

"These are three things which are rare indeed and are due to the Grace of God, namely Human birth, the longing for Liberation and the protecting care of a perfected sage." Vivekachud, v.3.

"What greater fool is there than the man who having obtained a rare human body, neglects to achieve the real end of this life?" V. 5.

"O foolish person, cease to identify thyself with this bundle of skin, flesh, fat, bones and filth and identify thyself instead with the absolute Brahman, the self of all, and thus attain to supreme peace." V. 161.

The Mooladhar chakra at the base of the spine, presiding over the earthly element holds the Kundalini coiled up.

The incarnated soul (jivatma) will have to go through all the worldly experience of childhood, adolescence, adult age influenced by family, education, social surroundings, and karmic past heritage before the soul starts searching within for an answer, an exit path.

Spiritual awakening always comes when time is ripe. To that call of the heart, the Lord will respond, in the form of the Guru, and give a new birth to the longing aspirant. As the Kundalini is the key to open spiritual doors, The Guru holds it, turns it and controls its motions. Kundalini and the Guru are one, working in perfect harmony.

The one who when coiled up was the cause of bondage now through Grace becomes a source of emancipation. Without the touch of the perfect Master, her awakening at the lowest Chakra is dangerous, as it stands amid great Mavic (deluding) influence. At this point duly awakened through her seed letters and root mantras, her divine symbols, the. Kundalini will enter new vibrating currents, hissing like a serpent nourished by pranas. At this level, she will set into motion different Yogic Kriyas, having for prime purpose the purification of the physical and vital sheaths, and new life currents will be cleared of all impurities. However, these experiences vary with aspirants.

As the Kundalini proceeds from the gross to the more subtle, the time taken for the piercing of the chakras depends upon the karmic past of the disciple, his capacity to receive the new Divine energy and the ability the Guru must lead the Divine Shakti upwards. The two lower chakras should be crossed over quickly as their piercing generates a lot of heat and increases sexual impulses.

Along with the physical Kriyas taking place at the beginning of practice to remove latent diseases and allow the energy to flow more freely, a gradual purification of the subconscious mind is also experienced. As we have observed in our description of the chakras, each centre corresponds to a certain level of consciousness, we find the lower human tendencies located from the root chakra up to the heart chakra, representing the physical, lower vital, vital and emotional beings.

The dualities inherent in our nature act as several blockages accumulated in our consciousness through' many life times. The Kundalini endowed with Deities, Seed letters, symbols, once awakened, will start her purificatory action, stimulated by the Guru's divine force, mantra recitation and meditation, and will bring two different types of experiences.

First, new divine sensations, feeling visions, experiences of peace, love and happiness, which are the results of the Grace of God, Guru and the inner Divinity now awakened. And second, as side effects, the performance of kriyas, asanas, pranayam, as bandhas, very negative feelings, and thoughts, arising from subconsciousness and reflect on the surface mind.

Therefore, the presence and guidance of a perfected Master are an absolute must in the beginning to go through all these experiences, protected and helped. Spiritual life is a constant duel between Good and Evil, the one trying to get hold of the other. Great dispassion and discrimination is constantly needed to avoid the several pitfalls coming on the way.

The Kundalini and all her deities protect so long as the aspirant conducts his practice in the right spirit following the injunctions received from his Guru; but they can become inimical once the elementary rules are broken. As it is often said spiritual life is like walking on the edge of a sharp sword. The first work of the Kundalini will be to perform a gross purification, at all levels, next she will have to transform the purified being into a still better medium capable of receiving higher energies, more subtle and go through deeper experiences. All this demands regular and constant spiritual practices; these steps one must go through; they cannot be crossed all at once. A long, patient progression must be respected; intense faith, devotion is required to conquer gradually the realms of emancipation.

Even when the six Chakras are pierced, the Shakti will not at once remain centred in the Brain; she will rise upwards and come down again; she will have to be stirred up constantly by Japa, Meditation and Contemplation, until our whole being accepts her as her own. During this long, silent, patient march, the outer world along with its multifaceted dualities, and magnetic attraction will act as a constant source of unbalance and gap, working often at the opposite of our practices, and aspirations.

This step, hard to cross, has made several seekers abandon their efforts and return to their previous conditions leaving unripe the fruit of their work. It is surely the time to remember the wisdom of the Great Seers, vanquishers of ignorance. Conquerors of Bliss, who crossed this earthly plane, moulding it to their need. The power of their realizations and Divinity will forever stimulate and encourage the true faithful seekers. No contemporary life can illustrate more vividly the victory of Spirituality than Shri Ramakrishna's, a life gifted with all kinds of Sadhanas and realizations of the very Grace of Mother Kundalini.

The Divine Mother he had so ardently longed for and worshipped in the temple of Kali at Dakshineshwar had become so alive within himself; he could see her, talk to her and hear the tingling of her anklets at night, while she was walking on the terrace overhanging the Ganges. It was the same Cosmic Mother who through Shri Ramakrishna's touch empowered Swami Vivekananda to de liver the Message of Universal Religion to the western world at the beginning of our century and plant the first seeds of Yoga and Vedanta in the Christian Lands.

By the Grace of his Divine Guru Shri Ramakrishna, son of the Merciful Mother, Swami Vivekananda had reached the summits of spiritual realization and accomplished a magnificent task all over the world despite his young age. Shri Ramakrishna had transformed him into a great devotee of the Holy Mother. On the day of his Maha-Samadhi, Swami Vivekananda, while he was descending the stairs of the shrine in the Ashram sang this beautiful song:

"Is Kali, my mother, really black?
The Naked one, though black seems
Lights the lotus of my heart.
Men call her black, but yet my mind

Will not believe that she is so:
Now She is White, now Red, now Blue;
Now She appears as Yellow too.
I hardly know who Mother is
Though I have pondered all my life:
Now Purusha, now Prakriti,
And now the void she seems to be.
To Meditate on all these things.
Confounds poor Kamalakant's wits."

As old as the Vedic time, The Divine Cosmic Mother conquered the Love and Devotion of all great saints and yogis. During the eighth century after Christ, the Great Jagad Guru Shri Adya Shankaracharya, reviver of the Vedic Dharma and Vedanta philosophy, wrote these beautiful verses dedicated ed at her Lotus Feet:

"Oh Gracious One, you are the sun
Which dispels the darkness of the unlettered?
You are the stream of consciousness
Ignorant for the unthinking,
You are the giving Chintamani stone
For the poor, to those drowned by the sea
Of births, you are the tusks of the Boar
Who rescued the earth from underwater." V. 3
"Oh! Auspicious one, worship rendered
To your feet becomes also the Worship
of the three Gods born of the three Gunas,
For these ever remain near your foot pedestal
With bent crowns and folded hands." V. 25

"Through the sight of self-surrender,
Let my prattle become a recitation of your name;
The movement of my limbs, gestures of worship;
My walk perambulation offering to you,
My lying down prostration to you;
Whatever I do for my pleasure, let it become
Transformed into an act of worship to you." V. 27
"You are the Mind, you are Ether,
You are Air, Fire, Water, and Earth.
You manifest yourself as the Universe,
There exists nothing other than you.
To transform yourself, who is consciousness,
Bliss, into the Universal body, you deem

Yourself the Young bride of the Auspicious one." V.35
"Oh! Queen of the Supreme God,
The learned ones have deemed you
As the Goddess of Learning, wife of the creator,
As the Goddess of Riches, wife of the protector,
As the daughter of the mountain,
The consort of the destroyer.
But you as a mysterious, illusory fourth power
With an inaccessible, infinite greatness
Dazzle the Universe." V. 97 - Saundarya Lahari.

Much more recently, the great Poet Seer of Modern India, Shri Aurobindo wrote this beautiful description of the Kundalini's

Awakening in his Epic Savitri. Just before the Death of her beloved husband Satyavan, Savitri calls upon The Mighty Mother to descend into herself,

"A Mighty movement rocked the inner space
As if a world were shaken and found its soul:
Out of the Inconscient's soulless mindless Night
A flaming Serpent rose released from sleep.
It rose to billow its coils and stood erect
And climbing mightily stormily on its way
It touched her centres with its flaming mouth.
As if a fiery kiss had broken their sleep.
They bloomed and laughed surcharged with light and bliss;
Then at the crown, it joined the Eternal's space.
In the flower of the head, in the flower of Matter's base,
In each divine stronghold and Nature-knot
It held together the mystic stream which joins
The viewless summits with the unseen depths,
The string of forts that make the frail defence
Safe guarding us against the enormous world;
All underwent a high celestial change:
Breaking the black inconscient's blind mute wall,
Effacing the circles of Ignorance,
Powers and divinities burst flaming forth;
Each part of the being trembling with delight
Lay overwhelmed with tides of happiness
And saw her hand in every circumstance
And felt her touch in every limb and call;

In the country of the Lotus of the head
Which thinking mind has made its busy space,
In the castle of the Lotus twixt the brows
Whence it shoots the arrows of its sight and will,
In the passage of the Lotus of the throat
Where speech must rise and the expressing mind
And the heart's impulse runs towards word and fact,
A glad uplift and a new working came.
The immortal's thoughts displaced earthbound view,
The immortal's thoughts on earth's drab idea and sense;
All things now bore a deeper heavenlier sense.
A glad clear harmony marked their truth's outline,
Re-set the balance and measures of the world.
Each Shape showed its occult design, unveiled
God's meaning in it for which it was made.
And the vivid splendour of his artist thought,
A Channel of the mighty Mother's choice,
The immortal's will take into its calm control
Our blind and erring government of life;
A loose republic once of wants and needs,
Then bowed to the uncertain Sovereign mind,
Life now obeyed a diviner Rule
And every act became an act of God.
In the kingdom of the Lotus of the heart
Love chanting its a pure hymeneal hymn
Made life and body mirrors of sacred joy
And all the emotions gave themselves to God.

In the navel lotus's broad imperial range.
Its proud ambitions and its master lusts
Were tamed into instruments of great calm sway
To do a work of God on earthly soil.
In the narrow nether center's petty parts
Its childish game of daily dwarf desires
Was changed into a sweet and boisterous play,
A romp of little gods with life in time.
In the deep place where once the Serpent slept,
There came a grip on Matter's giant powers
For large utilities in Life's little space;
A firm ground was made for Heaven's descending might.
(SAVITRI Book VII, Canto 5)

PART II

THE PRACTICE OF MAHA YOGA

(1) THE GURU

GURURUPĀYAH

The Guru is the means. (Śiva sūtra)

As we have already noticed in the first part; the practice of Kundalini Yoga is hard and complex; any attempts made to practice it on one's own are very risky, even dangerous. Only a Perfect Master, fully realized who knows all the intricacies of the path can initiate and guide the seeker on his journey. The ways by which Kundalini Yoga can be practiced are many. The Sadguru aware of the Karmic past of his disciple and his present capacities will choose for him the path most suitable to his character, and physical and mental abilities. Such a choice is a rare blessing and will ferry the disciple to the other shore.

The Guru is the only one able to control the mighty powers of the Kundalini and break the knots of Ignorance, blocking the further progress of the disciple. Therefore, the Guru is the means, their holder, the Great Bestower of Grace.

"As Human, the Guru is seen by the sinner;

As Divine, by the merciful."

– Kularnava Tantra-13

For the past two decades, In India as well as in the Western world, the number of so-called "Gurus" has been ever-increasing misleading the masses through their selfish and wealth-acquiring purposes. To such an extent that the word Guru, is often employed now as a synonym for Charlatan! Within no time the dreadful power of Ignorance wishes to annihilate thousands of years of Deep Esoteric tradition! But can a surface wave shake the depth of Time and Divinity?

Guru Gita says: "The syllable GU is darkness and the syllable RU is said to be Light. He by whose light (true knowledge) arise is known by the word GURU. GURU is indeed the supreme knowledge that swallows the Darkness born of Ignorance." v-23

The real understanding of the word Guru is far beyond the ordinary capacity of reason and human judgment. Although the word Guru is often used to refer to a human being, it misses its real meaning and confines itself just to an exterior outlook devoid of further reality.

Guru Gita further says:

"The Guru is Brahma. The Guru is Vishnu.

The Guru is Lord Shiva.

The Guru is the realized one, The Supreme God Head. Salutations to the Guru." v-32

As Brahma, the creator, the Guru gives new birth to the disciple, as Vishnu the preserver, the Guru protects, and guides the disciple along the hard path, and as Shiva the destructor, the Guru destroys and annihilates the knots of Ignorance having their roots in the Ego sense. The Guru is indeed the realized and living consciousness of Supreme Divinity which defies the three worlds.

The Guru is a principle (Tattva). It is that form of God, known as light, Truth Grace, knowledge, destroyer of impurities, giver of Liberation. The Guru in a Human form is the embodiment of the Truth realized, manifested in him, invoked through him. He abides in Pure

Divine consciousness and roams the earth bestowing his Grace on good seekers. He can in no way be assimilated with all those fakes who proclaim themselves to be spiritual guides and who, through the power of their ego wish only to increase the number of their disciples and get hold of their wealth. Such people will only end up in hell and drag their followers along with them.

The Guru belongs to an unbroken lineage of perfect Masters descending from the Lord Himself, who never cease to communicate and maintain the Eternal principles of truth, throughout the ages. The Guru is endowed with all features, sweet looking like a God, full limbed, happy of countenance, ease of access. He dissipates delusion and doubt and knows the past, present, and future. He is even-minded, highly solemn, stainless, ever content, steadfast, merciful, and generous. He is independent and focused within. He is devoid of anger, hatred, fear, and pain, free from ostentation, egoism, unattached to women, wealth bad company, and vice. Beyond dualities, always parting good from evil, he supremely conforms to Dharma (right conduct).

Equal in praise and criticism, detached, silent, merged in yoga, the inner self, he is endowed with the powers of mantras, and knows the functions of the chakras in the body. He is an expert in awakening and controlling the Kundalini Shakti. He is perfect in Hatha Yoga, Raja Yoga, Laya Yoga, Bhakti Yoga, Mantra Yoga, Yantra Yoga and Vendanta. He is capable of purifying all impurities and severing all desires in the disciple. He grants spontaneous joy and peace, regulates the disciple in his practice, removes his afflictions, and destroys his doubts, obstacles, and sins.

Ever compassionate he imparts Knowledge freely. He is liberated and, therefore, can liberate. He spreads his consciousness as the sandalwood tree spreads its fragrance all around. His mere touch transmutes the disciple, like the philosopher's stone. Like the tortoise, he nourishes his disciples on thought alone. His Divine glance burns up the sins of seekers like the rays of the sun. He is the prompter, the awakener, and the bestower of liberation. He is truly God Incarnate!

The Tantras and other scripture unanimously declare that no man can walk the Path unaided. One who may be qualified, still needs someone to launch him on the journey, to set up that power in him which will allow further progress, protect, and guide him against all obstacles so hard to overcome through ordinary human capacity. To avoid all falsehood produced by. Ignorance, the Ego, and its selfish desires, one must resort to a Guide, a Master, the Desireless one, who has already trodden the Path and achieved realization.

Self-surrender, faith, receptivity, the right spirit of inquiry, and freedom from preconceived notions and prejudices. humility, devotion, and thirst for liberation are the means a sincere seeker needs to approach an Enlightened teacher and allow the communication of Yoga to take place.

Shri Shankara clearly defines the true way of approach in his Viveka Chudamani: "Worshipping that Guru with devotion and approaching him, when he is pleased with prostration, humility, and service, he should ask him what he has got to know: 0 Master, O friend of those that bow to thee, thou ocean of mercy; I bow to thee, save me, fallen as I am into this sea of birth and death, with a straightforward glance of the eye, which sheds nectar-like grace supreme.

Save me from death, afflicted as I am by the unquenchable fire of this world-forest and shaken violently by the winds of an untoward lot, terrified and so seeking refuge in thee, for I do not know of any other man with whom to seek shelter." V.34, 35-36.

Although a perfect Guru can initiate anyone, he will take care to test the disciple in manyfold ways before imparting the Sadhana best suited for him. The more receptive and surrendered will be the disciple, The quicker will be his progress. One who is a heretic, dirty, addicted to vices, cunning, treacherous, disloyal to his Master, sinful, distrustful, ever-doubting, cruel, fond of quarrel, foolish, offensive or abusive; gluttonous and lustful, cowardly, crooked, will have great difficulty in winning the grace of the Master and progressing spiritually.

On the contrary, one who is devoted to Dharma (right conduct, religion), pure of mind steady in observances, truthful practice, gifted with faith and devotion, clean, afraid of sin, humble, liberal, grateful, endowed with auspicious features, positive in his activities, will soon be rewarded for his efforts and qualities.

Of course, all qualities and virtues cannot be acquired all at once; but it is in the interest of the disciple to cultivate them constantly, to free himself from bondage and become fit for Darshan (divine company and blessings) That is the whole of Sadhana.

(2) SHAKTIPAT-DIKSHA

THE INITIATION

"Initiation is the first ladder to the terrace of Liberation.'

– Paramananda Tantra.

Wild practice of Yoga cannot be in any way beneficial. Even if one has succeeded in awakening one's Kundalini, one will sooner or later definitely reach a stage of confusion and restlessness. The process of initiation is obtained to secure for the disciple, protection, permanent guidance, and a link with the Divine. Initiations surely differ in forms, effects, and purposes. We are here concerned with that form of initiation known as 'Shaktipat' in Sanskrit.

Pat meaning transference and Shakti, power. Thus, Shaktipat is the transference of Divine power performed by the perfect Guru on the disciple, aiming at the Awakening of the Kundalini. It is the highest form of initiation one can receive as it embraces all Yoga's, techniques and Shaktis. Only Enlightened Masters who have a perfect control of Prana, mind and Astral body can perform it. This process is very complex but highly simplified by the perfected ones for the sake of their disciples.

The Sadguru whose prana and mind vibrate with the highest waves of Divine consciousness can raise the vital energy in others. At the time of Shaktipat he transfers in the astral body of the disciple a current of psychic power, an astral fluid of high potentiality which will act simultaneously as an injection of power and magnetic effect drawing upward spontaneously the Dormant Kundalini of the initiate, therefore establishing a permanent astral link with the Master. The

Guru's body is fully permeated with Shakti, it is the power of the Lord himself working through him which now onwards, will protect the disciple, control the movements of his Kundalini and enable him to progress.

There are Four ways by which the Guru can confer Shaktipat.

The first form of initiation is called: "Sparsha Diksha". through touch.

The Guru touches the disciple at different levels; in the middle of the eye-brows, the top of the head, the heart, or the base of the spine. This is usually done by keeping his fingers on the disciple's head, to allow the Shakti to flow into the astral body.

The second form is through word or "Mantra Diksha".

The Guru has perfected the Mantra and made it alive, a conscious Divine force. This Mantra force awakens at once the Kundalini when whispered or recited before the disciple. The third form is called "Drik Diksha' or initiation through look. The Guru saturated with Shakti gazes at the disciple and transmits his power through his eyes.

The fourth form is called 'Manasa Diksha or Sankalpa Diksha' initiation by will power. The Guru merely wishes it and he initiates the disciple. These four methods can be used separately or combined according to the needs of the disciples. All are extremely potent and effective and have the same lasting effect. Sometimes Shaktipat is also received in Dream, it is one of the best forms of initiation.: Authorized disciples of the Guru can also perform Shaktipat, they work as medium for the Guru.

Certain restrictions must be observed regarding the giving of

Shaktipat. To allow a better action of the Shakti, the initiate is often asked to fast a day before initiation. People suffering from Asthma, Hysteria, piles, tuberculosis, anaemia, veneral diseases, infected scabies, weak heart, incurable diseases, women during their menses, must not be given Shaktipat.

The initiation can follow the accomplishment of certain preliminary rites, or be totally informal, according to the Guru's wish. A high degree of receptivity and faith is essential at the time of initiation. Although there is only one Shakti transferred to everyone, she will be felt differently and manifest herself in different ways.

Her manifestations are known as "Kriyavati', "Kalavati', Varnamayee, 'Vedhamayee'. The manifestation of the Kundalini on the plane of Hatha yoga is known as Kriyavati. Any real potent initiation by a realized Guru can be called Shaktipat.

The Transmission and thus Transformation must happen.

(3) KUNDALINI AWAKENING

The evolution of the Kundalini traversing the unfoldment of the five Kalas (phases) is known as Kalavati; it is Laya Yoga.

When the Kundalini is awakened through mantra recitation, she is known as Varnamayee. When the Kundalini enters the Sushumna and pierces the six chakras, she is known as Vedhamayee. The primary action of the Kundalini is purificatory, on the physical body and the pranic channels (Nadi-shuddi). For that she performs several Kriyas of Hatha yoga; asanas, bandhas, mudras and automatic pranayamas.

The Kundalini then crosses the 5 phases during her upward journey, this process of evolution of the self is known as Tattwa Shuddi (purification of principles). These 5 phases (Kalas) are known as, Nivritti, Pratishta, Vidya, Shanti, Shantyatita. Nivritti is the primary renunciation, purifying the existence of the cosmic egg. Pratishta is the establishment of renunciation, which leads to the equilibrium of the three gunas, the unmanifest (avyakta).

Through Vidya the knowledge of the self is acquired. Shanti leads to the highest principles, peace. Shantyatita (beyond peace) leads to the Goal. The Yogi gradually detaches himself from these principles and reaches the goal. Kalavati covers the field of forms, Varnamayee of names, the subject of mantra yoga. The process of piercing the chakras is known as Shat-chakra-vedhan; it is a part of Raja yoga. The Vedhamayee Kundalini primarily acts on the motor system, but indirectly affects the autonomous system and the sensory system.

These different manifestations of the Kundalini are commonly known as kriyas, and are all performed to remove impurities. These different aspects of Yoga succeed to each other according to the needs of the disciples; through different symptoms after Shaktipat. A throbbing of the lowest chakra (mooladhar) is felt. The whole-body shakes, trembles, hair stands on roots. The body moves to and fro, performs various types of asanas automatically, bandhas (yogic seats: Moolbandha, Uddiyanbandha, Jalandharbandha), different types of (spontaneous) pranayamas. Currents of prana (vital force) rise in the cerebrum, vibrations work all over the body. Sight is attracted towards the middle of the eyebrows, the eyeballs revolve, the tongue reverts, rises towards the palate.

The whole body is shaken by energy. Deformed sounds are uttered as well as mantras. Different kinds of sounds are heard. Lights, symbols, gods, goddesses, frightening scenes are envisioned. A feeling of intoxication with peace and joy is felt. At this time, one must understand that, though those manifestations differ from the idea we have of spirituality, they are needed stages in the practice.

Those kriyas must not be stopped or controlled, they must be allowed to perform their primary work which is essential for further progress. These effects of Shaktipat vary with individuals, It happens that at the time of initiation nothing is felt, only later will the action of the Shakti be experienced.

The Jnanarnava Tantra beautifully describes the potency. of Shaktipat :

"The touch of the hand of the Guru destroys the impurities of the world and converts the base metal into gold."

Shaktipat is indeed a rare blessing, the very manifestation of God's grace. This science of Shaktipat also known as Maha Yoga, Siddha Yoga, Poorna Yoga, Kundalini Yoga etc... is in no way a new discovery; it has been known to High initiates from time immemorial.

(4) GURU and DISCIPLE'S RELATIONSHIP

We find in the Yoga Vasistha how the great Guru Vasistha performed Shaktipat on Lord Rama. These techniques were also known to the ancient Greeks, and Egyptians. Jesus the Christ often performed Shaktipat.

Lord Chaitanya Maha Prabhu was also such an accomplished master. More recently Shri Ramkrishna revived these techniques; most of his chief disciples also initiated in this way. Bagawan Ramana Maharishi, Shri Aurobindo, Bhagawn Nityananda, the Mother, Paramhansa Yogananda, Swami Shivananda, Swami Muktananda, Anand Mayi Ma, our own Master Dhyan Yogi Madhusudandas, Swami Vishnu Tirth etc... all performed Shaktipat. Now here are a few accounts of Shaktipat:

Shri Rama Krishna initiates Swami Vivekananda.

"During his second visit to the Master, Narendra (Swami Vivekananda) had an even stranger experience. After a minute or two Shri Ramkrishna drew near him, in an ecstatic mood, muttered some words, fixed his eyes on him and placed his right foot on Naren's body. At this touch Naren saw, with eyes open, the walls, the room, the temple garden, nay the whole world vanishing and even himself disappearing into a void."

At the end of Shri Ramkrishna's life, when he was very ill, he came down his room one afternoon to have a walk in the garden. After listening to a devotional hymn sung by a devotee, the Master went into a deep samadhi. When his mind had partially returned to external consciousness, he gazed affectionately at his devotees and said: "What else shall I tell you!" May your spiritual consciousness awake! As soon as he had pronounced these words, all devotees felt a flow of infinite Bliss moving within themselves. All exclaimed: "Glory to Ramkrishna, glory to Ramkrishna and bowed down to him. The Master still in a high divine state, touched them one by one saying: "May you be all enlightened. From that touch, the devotee felt a magnificent spiritual awakening. Some went into meditation, others were dancing with joy, others were crying and the Master stood looking at them in a great joy."

The account of our Master's initiation. This took place after our Masters first meeting with the Kaupin clad Yogiraj Shri Parameshwardasji at Mount Abu.

"I sat in front of him and I was ordered to close my eyes. As soon as I closed my eyes the saint kept his hand over my head for about five minutes. At that time, I felt as if my body was on fire and I visualised wonderful and inexplicable light. I had lost the holy consciousness and I experienced divine pleasure, and must have remained in that condition for about 25 minutes." He further describes the full awakening of his Kundalini:

"While I was chanting Ram, I lost my body consciousness within five minutes and felt as if my body was filled with Divine Light and with a cyclonic thunder blast my prana after meeting the Apana started ascending from Muladhara, gradually. I had a feeling of suffocation and I just could not exhale. The part left by Kundalini during ascent, felt numb. I was scared and wondered whether I would die. With the ascent of Kundalini and piercing of chakras, there was a peculiar pleasure, but as this was accompanied by numbness in the lower parts and suffocation, I was scared to death and wondered whether I would come down to the normal plane. I still remember, that after traversing above the level of the neck, there was decrease in the thoughts. After some time, when the Kundalini travelled above the eye brows, I felt as if my skull was bursting with bliss and as if bliss was sprinkling like a fountain through the hair follicles of my head as if I was submerged in the sea of bliss. I have no words to describe this condition. Not only had I never experienced such super natural bliss and magnificent light, but had not even heard about the same! I realized that I was in that state for two and half hours, that the awakening of Kundalini and its subsequent ascent to Sahasrar as described by Yogis must be the same." (Message to Disciples)

We also find some accounts of Shaktipat in the Holy Bible. After the crucifixion, Lord Jesus appeared to the disciples: 'Once more Jesus said to them, peace be upon you; I came upon an errand from my father and now I am sending you out in my turn. With that, he breathed on them and said to them, receive the Holy Spirit." - John.

When the day of Pentecost came round, while they were ail gathered in unity of purpose, all at once a sound came from Heaven like that of a strong wind blowing and filled the whole house where they were sitting. Then appeared to them what seemed to be tongues of fire, which parted and came to rest on each of them; and they were filled with the Holy spirit and began to speak in various languages, as the spirit gave utterance to each."

That was how the disciples got empowered to continue Lord Jesus's Mission. - Act of Apostles.

Swami Vivekananda says:

"When the divinely appointed teacher comes, serve him with childlike confidence and simplicity, freely open your heart to his influence and see in him God feasted. Those who come to seek truth with such a spirit of Love and veneration, to them the Lord of Truth reveals the most wonderful things truth, goodness, and beauty.'

"The only medium through which spiritual force can be transmitted is Love.' (Bhakti Yoga)

What matters in Divine life is the communion or spiritual relationship between Guru and disciple. Spiritual progress closely follows that relationship. In fact, it is the highest relationship one can attain in a human life, but surely the hardest to perfect. The Guru selflessly enters the disciples' self and from now onward, their fate will be correlated.

Though the Guru remains ever detached, he constantly helps the disciples to cross the many obstacles coming on the way. He does not hesitate to lighten the disciple's burden by taking physical pains on his own body. Adhering to his principles he will never abandon the disciple, but always work in his interest.

Before the ever-perfect attitude of the Master, the disciple has the hard task to please him, to make himself worthy of such blessings. In no way he knows, he can repay what he owes to his Master; he must be ready to face the changing moods of the Guru, accept them work with them to be free. The Grace of the Guru is ever present; but only when the disciple's grace unfolds in the form of complete surrender and receptivity in a mirror like way; that Yoga, the Aim of Sadhana is achieved. The Disciple bows to the Guru and the Guru to the disciple in an unbroken flow of pure non-dual consciousness.

(5) THE IMPORTANCE OF BHOOT-SHUDDHI

A mantra is a force composed of certain letters infused with the power and realisation of the Guru, which, when given to the disciple at the time of initiation produce certain effects on the consciousness of the receiver. Usually after the receiving of Shaktipat, a mantra called the Bhoot shuddhi, must be recited a certain number of times for a certain number of days, in the right manner to produce fruition. We will come back later to the subject of the mantra with a deeper study.

We are at present concerned with that process called the Bhoot Shuddhi, meaning: purification of the elements'; it can be achieved through mantra, certain rites or pranayama. As we have already studied in the chapter on the Chakras; at each level of consciousness in the chakras works a tattva or element. Those Tattvas are earth, water fire, air and ether. They have a definite action at those centres and are associated with physical, vital, mental, and psychic functions. These layers of consciousness present in our subtle and causal bodies, have their correspondents in the atmosphere around us, directed by the elemental's forces of Universal Nature, which have a constant play and action upon our own inner elements and consciousness.

Everyone is subject to such influences, which highly determine our character and life in this world. They are like the different colours and attributes of our karmas and their actions, which limit and degrade. The Bhoot-Shuddhi is the indispensable preliminary discipline one must undertake before starting any spiritual work. It is the very first step of sadhana. It aims at clearing, purifying the atmosphere within and around the initiate, to free him from all elemental influences which stop his evolution. It acts as Nadi Shuddi purification of the ducts in the subtle body and Tattva Shuddhi, purification of the elements.

The action of the Bhoot Shuddhi mantra is extremely subtle; it gradually refines the layers of our subconscious, vital and emotive being, allowing the divine power received during Shaktipat to accomplish its task. Unless this Bhoot Shuddhi is accomplished we cannot perceive our Self as it is, and commune with our own inner deity. It has two kinds of actions: First to clean our consciousness from its impurities, and negativities at different levels and next to install instead the different divine powers.

The Bhoot Shuddhi mantra should only be received from one's Guru and recited according to his instructions. Our Master relates what he was told when he first met his own Master: "Do you know that cloth cannot be dyed without cleaning it first!

"I was impressed by his nectar like sweet voice and requested him to explain what he meant. He asserted that without proper Bhoot-Shuddi the goal cannot be reached by any means."

It is a very potent and blissful mantra which allows further progress in meditation and mantra sadhana. Prior to starting of the Sangarsan Puja (a lengthily puja performed by Sri Vidyaists) after having lighted and worshipped the Divine Lamp , a very effective and powerful Mantras called Bhut Suddhi , the purification of the five elements is given. It can be used through a specific Pranayama or as Mantra Anusthan. It is must and the main mantra for entering the Antaryaga, the inner worship, inner Sadhana. The success of further Sadhana depends on this Mantra only, which is the awakener and the expander of the kundalini Sakti. My first Guru always used to say "whenever you are stuck on the path, recite this Mantra". it has been verified all throughout my life.

But the Mantra which was given by Guruji had only two Bijas: yam (for the Air element) and Ram (for the fire element). The one used in Sri Vidya covers up the five elements but is not normally meant for Mantra japa, only to be used with Pranayama. But because a single round of Pranayama cannot make this Mantra so effective, I believe some Anusthan should be performed to activate the potent effect of this Mantra, which is the very root of Kundalini Yoga and of the purification of the five elements (Panca Makaras) and in which lies further success of the Patra Sadan Puja , prior to the Atma Pratistha and Matrika Nyasas.The introductory Mantra of the Bhut Suddhi of Sri Vidya goes this :

ॐ ऐं ह्रीं श्रीं भूतशृङ्गाटात् त् शिरः सुषुम्णापथेन

जीव - शिवं परम शिव पदे योजयामि स्वाहा ।

Om aim hrim srim bhuta srngatat sirah susumna pathena

Jiva Shivam parama Shiva pade yojayami svaha

Aim, Hrim, Srim are the kundalini Bijas (Guruji`s Bhut Suddhi does not include these three Bijas). The Jivatman residing in one`s heart connects to the Citta Nadi (the Channel of the causal body) from which arises the original Prana of the Soul, the basis of all life. It governs all the channel intimately related to the Susumana, the governing channel of the subtle body. The Kundalini awakens to flow through the Susumna only. When the Citta Nadi flows within our energy gets directed within for internal spiritual transformation. It leads to the purification and the energization of all other Nadis, leading to the opening of the Chakras with all their potentials. The Citta Nadi is desire based but detachment allows it to flow within. The sexual energy is reversed by the awakening of the Kundalini. It then takes an upward course through the Susumna, that is why the Kundalini is so important in Sri Vidya. Sexual desire is as much the root of delusion and worldly life as the root of sublimation and liberation through Kundalini Vidya Sakti. That is what the Tantras and Sri Vidya teach. Use the poison to cure the poison.

The Citta Nadi is closely related to Vata, itself connected to Prana, to the heart and the mind. So the Citta Nadi takes a part of the heart seed atom which represents the Jivatman at the Muladharaa, from where the Kundalini will flow upwards through the Susumna, piercing the seven Chakras (Chakra Bhedan) and dissolving one element into the other (Tattvalaya).

The second Mantra of the Bhut Suddhi of Sri Vidya says:

ॐ ऐं ह्रीं श्रीं यं लिङ्गशरीरं (or संकोच शरीर)

शोषय शोषय स्वाहा

Om Aim Hreem Shreem Yam Linga Shariram (Or Sankoch Sariram)

Sosay Sosay Swaha

Yam is the Vayu Bindu (Air) in the heart Chakra. Sri Vidya says Sankoca Sariram (withering body) but we can use Linga sariram (subtle body). Sosaya means dry up.

The third Mantra is thus:

ॐ ऐं ह्रीं श्रीं रं सङ्कोचशरीरं

दह दह पच पच स्वाहा

Om Aim Hreem Shreem Ram Sankoch Sariram

Daha Daha Paca Paca Swaha

Ram is the Agni Bija (Fire) in the Nabhi Chakra. It is supposed to burn up the withering causal body and reduce it to ashes (paca paca).

The fourth Mantra goes thus:

ॐ ऐं ह्रीं श्रीं वं परंशिवममृतं

वारशय वारशय स्वाहा

Om aim hreem shree vam param shiva amrutam

Varsaya varsaya svaha

Vam is the Water BIja (Jal Tattva). Once the two bodies, subtle and causal have been dried up and burnt up, Vam Bija of the svadhisthan which is also in the Sahasrar is supposed to shower (Varsa) nectar (Amrta) on the purified bodies rejuvenating the whole system by endocrine secretions.

The fifth Mantra says:

ॐ ऐं ह्रीं श्रीं लं शम्भवशरीरं

उत्त्पादय उत्त्पादय स्वाहा

Om aim hreem shreem lam sambhava sariram

Utpadaya utpadaya svaha

Lam, the Earth Bija (the Solid Bija) is supposed to create (Utpadaya) a new Shiva body (Sambhava Sariram)

And the sixth and last Mantra goes thus:

ॐ ऐं ह्रीं श्रीं हंसः सोऽहं

अवतर अवतर शिवपदत जीवं

सुषुम्णा पथेन प्रविश मूलश्रुङ्गातम्

उल्लस उल्लस ज्वल ज्वल प्रज्वल प्रज्वल

हंसः सोऽहं स्वाहा

Om aim hreem shreem ham sah so ham

Avatara avatar Shivapadat jivam

Susumna pathena pravisa mula sringatam
Ullasa ullasa jvala jvala prajavala prajvala
Hamsah so ham svaha
(For the record, the last mantras of Guruji`s Bhut Suddhi was:

ॐ परम् शिव सुषुम्णा पथेन मूलश्रुङ्गातम्

उल्लस उल्लस ज्वल ज्वल प्रज्वल प्रज्वल

हंसः सोऽहं स्वाहा

Om paramShiva susumna pathena mula srigatam
Ullasa ullasa jvala jvala prajavala prajvala
Hamsah so ham svaha

Avatara means descent, that is manifestation, Shivapadat are foot soldiers' devotees of Shiva, Pravisa is enter, Ullasa shine or delight, Jvala blaze, Prajvala blaze forth descent of the supramental in the body. The Mantra says the Jiva who has become shiva redescends as a form of the Divine (Shiva) down to the root Chakra. Blaze, blaze be in flame as the Divine Self. Here we offer the final oblation with the Hamsah Mantra. Just as rice with the husk is called paddy so also ParaShiva with Avidya superimposed gets the name of JivaShivam. Only if this triple body is burnt up can unification with Parashiva be attained. Perfection, omniscience, contentment, omnipresence, omnipotence shine in full splendor. The Jivatman goes its real life only due to Shiva and the Sadhaka becomes Shiva only. The continuance of the Atman in this state is known as Atma Pratistha.

In his Saundarya Lahari Adi Shankaracharya repeats the same idea and practice:

महीं मूलाधारे कमपि मणिपूरे हुतावहं
स्थितं स्वधिस्थाने हृदी मरुतमकाशमुपरि
मनोऽपि भ्रूमध्ये सकलमपि भीत्वा कुलपथं
सहस्रारे पद्मे सह रहसि पत्या विहरसे

Mahim Muladharae kamapi manipure hutavaham
Sthitam svadhisthane hrdi maruta makasamupari
Manopi bhrumadhye sakalamapi bhitva kulapatham
Sahasrare padme saha rahasi patya viharase

After having traversed the entire path of Kundalini, the element Earth in Muladhara , water in Svadhisthan , Fire in Manipur , Air in Anahat , Ether above the Visuddhi and the mind in Ajna between the eyebrows , you sport with your ord in secret in the thousands petalled lotus of Sahasrar.

Then the Acarya describes the enlightened descent of the Kundalini back to Muladhara in the following verse:

सुधाधारासारैश्चरणयुगलान्तर्विगलितैः
प्रपञ्चं सिञ्चति पुनरपि रसाम्नायमहसः
अवाप्य स्वां भूमिं भुजगनिभमध्यौस्तवलयं
स्वमात्मानं कृत्वा स्वपिषि कुलकुण्डे कुहरिणि

Sudha dharasaraiscarana yugalantar vigalitaih
Prapancam sincanti punarapi rasamnaya mahasah
Avapya svam bhumim bhuja ganibha madhyausta valayam
Svamatmanam krtva svapisi kulakunde kuharini

Oh, glorious one, drenching all the veins with the nectar dripping from your feet, from the dizzy heights you descend to your abode and turning yourself into a serpentine coil , sleep in the fire hole of the Lotus root of the Muladhara. Then Adi Shankaracarya describes the Sri Chakra, the symbolic abode of the supreme power in the next verse:

चतुर्भि श्रीकण्ठे: शिवयुवतिभि: पञ्चभिरपि
प्रभिन्नाभि: शम्भोर्नवभिरपि मूलप्रकृतिभि:
चतुश्चत्वारिंशद्वा सुदलकलास्रात्रिवलय
त्रिरेखाभिः सार्ध तव शरणकोणा: परिणताः

Chaturbhi srikanthaih Shivayuvatibhih pancabhirapi
Prabhin nabhih sambhor navabhir api mula prakrtibhih
Catus catvarim sadva sudala kalas ratrivalaya
Trirekhabhih sardha tava saranakonah parinatah

Oh, supreme power, the angles of your abode becomes forty four in number with your wheels of auspiciousness (Shivakona) , five different wheels of power (Saktikona) , nine basic roots of nature (the nine Avaranas or Chakras) and the three encircling lines (virtual Trilaya) encasing eight and sixteen petals (the two lotuses of the Sri Chakra).

The Acharya considers the Sri Yantra only after the descent of the Kundalini back into Muladhara becomes Divine to worship the Divine, in other words, get purified to unite with the Divine. This is the same as the descent of the Supramental in Shri Aurobindo`s thinking. This yoga is a Jnanayaga. It is an inner sacrifice by means of knowledge, there is no need for any external accessories.

(6) YAMAS - NIYAMAS

We have seen how our whole being is constantly subject to a play of different forces, whose effects get deeply imprinted over our character, physcial, vital, emotional, and mental habits. They are activated by our past karmas, surroundings, heredity, education, civilization, present actions, and desires acting without respite over our consciousness, preventing us knowing and experiencing what we really are. What we perceive of ourselves is always false or rather limited!

To come to the point to wish to live a spiritual life is surely a great achievement in human life, to obtain a spiritual master a still greater one, but still greater is to be able to Practice successfully his precepts and teachings. It is observed that once we start any spiritual practice, following strictly a Master's direction, we have to come across all sorts of oppositions, negativities as if our whole being, rejected all these practices, refused to be tamed by diviner laws. All these automatisms of our character blindly revolt themselves. It is indeed a hard stage to cross.

Certain people claim that character cannot be changed by any means. But the science of Yoga teaches that the building up of a new character is an absolute necessity for spiritual life. We have already stated the importance of the Bhoot Shuddhi; to give a greater potency to this process, we must observe certain rules and regulations which will channelize our practice into the right evolutionary path. Our character can be transformed only by the building up of a new character. For that purpose, we will have to undergo a new moral training, a new understanding of ourselves, a new way to live our lives according to spiritual precepts. Those are the very steps described in the science of Raja Yoga and Vedanta philosophy. Those rules and regulations are known as "Yama' and 'Niyama'. Swami Vivekananda says:

"The Yama and Niyama are moral trainings, without these as the basis no practice of Yoga will succeed, without these it will never bear fruit." AHIMSA (non-violence), SATYA (truthfulness), ASTEYA (non-stealing), BRAHMACHARYA (continence), APARIGRAHA (non-receiving) are the five Yamas.

SHAUCH (purity), SANTOSH (contentment), TAPAS (penance), SWADHYAYA (study of the scriptures), ISHWARPRANIDHAN (complete surrender to God) are the five Niyamas:

(1) We shall not hurt anyone by thought, words and deeds: that is Ahimsa. By its practice one gets rid of all enmity and achieves quick results in any field.

(2) We shall not lie by thought, word and deeds: This is known as Satya. Whatever you say, or think, will come true. All ambitions will be fulfilled.

(3) We shall not steal anything or desire something belonging to someone else: that is Asteya. Its practice brings all wealth.

(4) We shall abide by Brahmacharya which means continence, cellibacy (physcial and mental). It is a very impotant step in the practice of Yoga. Without it no transformation of our character and being can be achieved. It increases bodily and mental energies, protects and leads to the higher stages of Samadhi. It is very essential to allow the good working of the Kundalini after Shaktipat.

(5) We shall also abide by Aparigraha which literally means non-receivings, as far as possible we should remain independent and avoid being under anybody's obligation. During the course of spirtual practice, receiving gifts often means receiving the evils of the giver. Through non-receiving we purify our minds and we get memory of our past lives.

After the five Yamas, let us consider the five Niyamas.

(1) **Shauch** means purity. It should be established internally as well as externally. By this discipline we gradually become free from body identification and avoid the company of impure people who interfere with our practice. It is extremely useful and protective, it awakes our sattvic being (inner purity) and brings cheerfulness.

(2) **Santosh** is contentment. We must limit our necessities and be happy with whatever circumstances God puts us into. It brings the best kind of happiness into the mind. It is the healer of all evils. Undisturbed in adverse conditions. We are free from cares and anxieties. We enjoy the peace and joy of the inner self.

(3) **Tapas** is the power of the determined will working for self-realization. The different kinds of austerities are its means. We must

be regular in food and work control our character and senses, as a result our psychic fire destroys all impurities and leads to physical and vital perfection.

(4) **Swadhyaya** means Study. We should regularly study the scriptures, chant mantras, perform japa (mantra repetition with faith and devotion. It leads to the union and visualization of one's own chosen deity (Ishtadeva).

(5) **Ishwarpranidhan** means complete self-surrender to God. We must realize the unreal nature of the ego sense and merge our self with God, taking refuge in him. By this sacrifice, resignation to the Lord, perfection in Samadhi is achieved.

These rules and regulations may appear to the profane modern man as mere religious propaganda. People usually expect extraordinary psychic experiences from spiritual life; and they are reluctant to make efforts and perform austerities.

To live a wild life and intend to achieve the Goal of Yoga is impossible!

When you build a house, first the foundations are to be made strong, those are the Yamas and Niyamas; without them the rest of the house will soon fall into ruins.

If, on the contrary, you observe them regularly with faith and perseverance, quick results will be gained and the goal achieved.

Viveka (discrimination), Vairagya (dispassion), Sama (calmness), Dama (Self-control), Titiksha (forbearance). Shraddha (faith), Bhakti (devotion), Satsang (company of the holy), Karuna (compassion) and Mumuksuta (yearning for freedom) are the further precepts to be Practiced on the spiritual path.

(7) FAITH, DEVOTION, ETC.

We must have yearning for freedom, a desire to free ourselves, to know our true nature, for that association with the wise, Satsang, serves as a boat to cross this terrible ocean of mundane existence. The company of Sages, of the Guru, even for a moment is highly beneficial; it destroys sins, elevates the Mind. Those who possess the divine virtues by their mere presence spread them all around like the fragrance of flowers. These blessings, obtained by the 'Darshan' of saints, grant discrimination, we become able to understand what is real in life, what is unreal, what must be done what must be avoided. It channels our practice and puts clear steps on our way. It awakes in us renunciation, the desire to give up all transitory enjoyments, being the cause of pains and miseries.

We become more and more detached towards this evanescent world and only seek right company and right conduct. Our whole consciousness gets transformed, we acquire a firm judgment, faith, we realize that the teachings of the scriptures the instructions of the Guru are true and definitely it conductive to progress and emancipation. We experience that there is no need to run here and there for new teachers, new scriptures, that sticking to one path quickly grants the expected reward. The more faith is established in us, the more devotion we gain; we feel that the only one to be loved is God, the only Goal to be achieved is truth.

"That divine love is nothing less than the immortal bliss of freedom, which comes unsolicited by the grace of God and by self-sacrifice. The man who gains Devotion, realizes his perfection and divinity becomes thoroughly contented. He is free from desire, grief, hatred, he becomes intoxicated and fascinated, completely immersed in the bliss of the self.

"Only love of the absolute, eternal truth is the greatest; this love indeed is the greatest." Says the divine sage, Narada.

Empowered with the blessings of discrimination, dispassion, faith, devotion, the disciple's mind rests steadfastly on its goal. Serenity, Calmness of mind, allows the bearing of all afflictions, frees from anxiety and lament. Forbearance is achieved, the sense organs come under control, devitalized before sense objects. This self-control gives absolute freedom, dauntless strength and energy (virya), friendliness (maitri) and compassion (karuna).

"When the mind is at peace and the heart leans to the supreme truth, when all the disturbing thought-waves in the mind stuff have subsided and there is an unbroken flow of peace, the heart is filled with the bliss of the absolute, when the truth has been seen in the heart, then this very world becomes an abode of bliss." Teachings of Guru Vasishta to Lord Rama in the Yoga Vasistha.

(8) OBSTACLES TO THE PRACTICE

The Kundalini Upanishad clearly describes the obstacles to the practice of Yoga. Which are blockages holding our physical, vital, and mental consciousness under wrong habits.

The **first** is sleeping during day time.

The **second** is late vigils at night.

If you invert the normal course of nature, you will gradually disturb the metabolism of the body and the functions of the autonomous system, which in turn will affect the body and character. The benefits of day-time cannot replace those of night time and vice and versa. Energies work differently during both periods; they should not be disturbed.

The **third cause** of disease is the excess of sexual intercourse. What we are seeking during Yoga practices is peace, self-control, physical and mental balance the taming of all energies, especially vital energies. Shaktipat initiation greatly helps the development of all those virtues. Excessive sex will ruin all those attempts, create an absolute confusion in the vital energies, restlessness in the brain. It can gradually disturb the work of the endocrine glands maintaining the good working of the whole system. The benefits of Shaktipat are wasted away.

Excessive walking amidst crowds is the **fourth obstacle.**

The activities of the body should be restrained, excessive walking must be avoided, it increases bodily needs and disturbs its vital functions. We are working and searching for peace, for that we need to protect ourselves with right judgement and action. The good vibrations we gradually store up during our practice, must not be wasted away. Our whole being becomes more and more subtle and sensitive, the presence of crowds with totally opposite vibrations of all kinds can surely affect our own.

The **fifth cause** of disease is the effect of unwholesome food.

The Yogi should consume very nutritious food in a controlled manner; this is known as Mitahara. Complete vegetarian food is essential for the good purification of the body. Fast and irregular partaking of food is forbidden. The practice of Yoga generates a lot of heat, the whole system needs light foods but rich ones, like milk, nuts, clarified butter, fruits, mung beans, wheat, rice etc a Regular and rich diet will give strength to the body and help to improve our practice.

The **sixth cause** of disease arises from constant obstruction to the passing of urine and faeces. This will disturb the whole digestive system, increase heat in the body, disturb blood circulation and gradually affect the brain, create hype acidity and gas in the body. The yogis always recommend before starting any practice to clear the bowels and pass urine. We have always to maintain a regular and controlled motion of the various functions of the body to keep them healthy and fit for practice.

Trying to control the vital energy (Prana) with force, thinking too much of it, is the seventh cause of disease. The control of Prana is very hard; pranayama must be Practiced gradually and under the instructions of a perfect Master. The body must accustom itself step by step to the increase and receiving of energies. Errors committed by breaking these rules, harm the autonomous system, the vital functions, and the brain. All these negative habits are very common in the modern man's life; they must be transformed first before starting any yogic practice. If we neglect these advices when disease comes, we will accuse Yoga of being their origin, and give up our practice. This is the **first obstacle** to Yoga.

The **second obstacle** will arise from doubt about the efficacy of such practices, we have seen how faith plays a prominent role in spiritual life. Doubt will act as a bad spirit on the confused and untrained mind, ruining little by little all our efforts. It will engender the **third obstacle,** carelessness, or a state of confusion. Body and mind being under the effect of disease created from wrong practices, have lost their balance, the capacity to act positively, to react with discrimination. This state of confusion leads to carelessness.

The **fourth obstacle** is indifference or sloth. The body and mind have now lost their sattvic constructive capacities; as a reaction a flow of Tamasic elements (inertia) will overcome the whole being, like the effect of drug of drink. The **fifth is** cessation.

The **sixth** is erroneous perception or delusion.

Concern with worldly affairs and sensual objects is the **seventh** obstacle. The whole being has been submerged by inertia as a reaction, Rajasic tendencies will rise more and more on the surface; the senses becoming restless, attachment and desires will multiply. Creating, anger, delusion, loss of memory, destruction of discrimination and self-control. Having totally lost faith in Yoga, the mind becomes more and more impure and restless.

Making fun of the practice, their secrecy is not kept; this is the **eighth obstacle. The ninth** is said to be non-aptitude for the understanding of the Truth of Yoga! So, the intelligent practitioner should avoid these nine obstacles through close investigation, discrimination and ad vice of the wise. No practice of Yoga is harmful provided one follows the rules prescribed and adheres to them with faith, discrimination and respect. If one avoids, negative habits, harmful company, hasty, judgments, this will help to build up Sattvic (pure) mental qualities, highly beneficial on the path of Yoga.

It is always very hard to construct something, it takes time, requires efforts, perseverance, and faith, while destroying it is very easy and quick. For that purpose, we need to settle rightly those two notions within real understanding and action. A lot of people give up their practice owing to above mentioned obstacles. It is a pity we are seeking truth and as a result we only come to ignorance. This is why the following of Yamas Niyamas is so important, to purify our character, strengthen it with positiveness, understanding and discrimination.

(9) HATHA YOGIC KRIYAS

We have already described that as an effect of Shaktipat initiation, several kinds of Kriyas are performed by the body during meditation. The most spectacular are the different yogic postures (asanas) and automatic pranayama. All these are accomplished by the divine Shakti, the mother of Yoga, for the purification of the ducts of vital energy, to remove diseases or psychosomatic disorders. Although the meditator does not know anything about these postures they are performed perfectly and with ease by the Shakti, who knows exactly which asanas are needed to train the body.

Usually, Asanas which form a part of Hatha Yoga have to be studied and Practiced for several years with a competent master before they become perfect and effective. The Divine Kundalini within no time grants the same results, even more perfect ones, free from the danger of harming the practitioner. In the same manner she performs automatic breathing exercises, which are so rhythmic and controlled, that one wonders how all this is done.

The active Kriyawati Kundalini, by using all these Hatha Yogic processes, gradually models the body and mind, prepares them against diseases and to receive higher energies coming in deeper states of meditation. The time of performance of those automatic kriyas also vary with disciples. Some do not experience any of those. It has been noted that several people who get such experiences are cured from: asthma, ulcer, obesity, head ache, abdominal pain, insomnia, anorexia and indifferent health.

Now apart from the observance of Yamas, Niyamas, mantra recitation, meditation, is it necessary to practice separately some asanas and pranayam after Shaktipat? Nor mally they should be very beneficial in helping to purify and strengthen the physical body, nervous system etc... but this all depends upon the instruction received by the master. All the kriyas of Hatha Yoga known as Shat Karma (dhauti, basti, neti, nauli, trataka, kapalabhati) as well as bandhas, asanas, pranayam must be learnt from a competent master. All these techniques are very powerful, as they awake and channel energies, but they must not interfere with the effects of Shaktipat, by increasing the amount of energy to an uncontrollable degree. However, the performance of certain asanas is beneficial before starting to meditate. They help a lot to achieve a steady posture, essential for meditation and mantra recitation.

Usually, Surya Namaskar or salutations to the sun, is to be

performed before asanas, it prepares for the practice of postures. Its twelve movements stimulate the whole body, make the spine flexible and strong, loosen the joints and muscles and help to coordinate the breath. Surya Namaskar stimulates the endocrine glands, blood circulation, the respiratory and digestive systems. It must be performed with proper rhythm, taking care to breathe harmoniously with each movement.

After completion 'Shavasan or the corpse pose must be done for a few minutes to allow the breath and blood circulation to return to normal. After that one can practice Trikonasana (three angle pose). This asan is very good for the spine, it tones the spinal nerves, the abdominal organs, relieves from constipation, increases appetite, it helps a better digestion, lightens body. It is very beneficial to lengthen the legs. Usually, three kinds of Asanas are Practiced. First in standing posture, secondly in sitting posture, thirdly in lying posture. We have already prescribed the performance of Surya Namaskar and Trikonasana, which are standing postures. Next it is very important to learn to master a good sitting posture. 5 sitting postres are commonly taught.

(1) Padmasana (lotus pose), (2) Siddhasan (perfect pose), (3) Svastikasana (auspicious pose), (4) Sukhasana (easy pose), (5) Vajrasana (admention pose). To allow the Kundalini Shakti to awake a good sitting posture must be Practiced.

The spine, the head, neck trunk are to be kept erect in one straight line. The body must not be contracted. The posture must be easy and comfortable, to allow a prolonged concentration. It is very beneficial to stick to the practice of one posture only and master it, padmasana, siddhasana, are harder to practice, Sukhasana is good enough for meditation These asanas increase the digestive five fire gives good appetite, removes Rheumatism helps the vital energy to flow in a better way, to stabilize the three humours in the body, strengthen the nerves of the legs and thighs improve concentration.

Pashchimottanasana (forward 'bend), is one of the classic postures: taught in various Hatha Yogic treatises. Its performance helps the vital breath to flow through the Sushumna Nadi in the spine. It rouses the Gastric fire, strengthens the muscles and nerves of the back, reduces obesity, and stimulates all the abdominal viscera, kidneys, liver, and pancreas. It increases the peristalsis of the bowels and removes constipation, dyspepsia, gastritis, lumbago, and myalgia, It cures piles, and diabetes. The whole autonomous nervous system is toned up and kept healthy.

Next to it **Vajrasan** (the adamantine pose) can be Practiced. It makes the spine firm and strong. This pose, is often used by Buddhists to meditate. It is very good for the muscles of the legs. It removes sciatica, flatulence and helps the stomach to work. It stimulates the place where all the ducts meet. Practiced for 15 minutes after taking food it helps digestion and removes dyspepsia.

Next comes **Gomukhasana** (cow face posture) and Ardha Matsyendrasana. Gomukhasana looks like the face of a cow, it removes rheumatism in the legs, sciatica, piles, indigestion, dyspepsia. It helps to maintain a good health and celibacy. **Ardha Matsyendrasana** derives its name from the Rishi Matsyendranath, who by the grace of Lord Shiva was transformed from a fish form into a perfect yogi. By this asana the spine is twisted through lateral movements; it keeps it elastic and massages the abdominal organs. It cures lumbago, tones up the sympathetic system increases the digestive fire, activates the pancreas, it awakes the Kundalini. After this short series of sitting postures come the lying down postures.

First in the series comes **Matsyasan** (fish pose) it is supposed to help to float on water easily. It regulates the thyroid gland and is very useful against respiratory problems, like asthma, bronchitis, etc. It removes constipation and nourishes the muscles and nerves of the back.

Next to it comes **Sarvangasana** (all members pose) with the head down and feet up. It is surely one of the best asanas most beneficial. It nourishes the thyroid gland allowing thus a good functioning of all the organs. Its inverted position makes it a good blood tonic and nourishes the spine. It is beneficial for varicose veins, constipation, and respiratory diseases, bladder problems. It also removes dyspepsia and gastro intestinal disorders. It awakes the Kundalini and increases the digestive fire. It is very useful to keep up celibacy.

Just following it is **Halasana** (plough pose) which amplifies the effect of Sarvangasana. It brings a large quantity of blood into the spinal roots of the nerves. It makes the spinal Colum soft and elastic. It tones and braces the abdomen muscles, rectal muscles, removes constipation, obesity, glum enlargement of the liver and the spleen. It also tones the kidneys and pancreas.

We have started the series with Matsyasan, but it can be Practiced after the other two. The next series starts with **Bhujangasana** (cobra pose). It is Practiced with the front part of the body lying on the ground. This asana bends the spine backwards. It awakes also the Kundalini. It relieves back pain, lumbago, constipation, increases appetite. It is very beneficial for ladies.

Supplementing Bhujangasana comes **Salabhasan** (locust pose). It improves digestion, removes gastric disorders, constipation, dyspepsia. It tones up the abdomen, liver, pancreas, kidneys, and increases the digestive fire.

Salabhasana can be followed by **Dhanurasana** (bow pose) which still increases its effects. These three asanas complement each other.

Before completing the practice of these asanas; **Sirshasana** (head standing pose) should be performed. It is known as the king of asanas. It is very good for the brain, which receives plenty of blood and vital energy. It increases memory, brightens the psychic faculties, and awakens the Kundalini.

It is beneficial for nearly all kinds of diseases; it is a powerful blood purifier. It helps a lot the practice of celibacy. It improves concentration and meditation. But it must be Practiced with due care and the guidance of a competent master. Too long standing on the head must be avoided. It is not suitable for certain type of people. As much time spent on the head should be spent in the reverse position standing straight. After it Savasana (corpse pose) must be Practiced, to ensure complete relaxation of all the muscles, normal and natural flow of blood and energies. Well-Practiced it helps meditation.

We have described here only very few but important postures, which can be daily Practiced. Asanas are supposed to be as many in number as there are species of living beings in this world 8400 000 according to Lord Shiva. 84 are the best, usually 32 are taught. For more instructions about them several detailed books are written on the subject. The main thing to remember is that they must be learnt gradually under the guidance of a perfect master, who knows all the rules related to them. The first and foremost rule necessary is pure vegetarian diet and balanced life. Without them, asanas can become dangerous and ineffective.

These asanas can be helpful for the practice of meditation and other spiritual disciplines. They train the body, remove diseases, improve the steadiness of posture and the different flows of energy.

But they are not an end in themselves in Maha Yoga. After the performance of Yoga Asanas, the practice of **Pranayamas** is advised. Several kinds of pranayamas are described in the Hatha Yogic treatises: Kapalbhati, Suryabheda, Ujjayi, Sitali, Sitkari, Bhastrika, Bhramari, Murchcha, Plavini and Kevala Kumbhaka."

They form a very advanced part of Hatha Yogic practices, each fulfilling a special purpose. They cannot be learnt on one's own! Total guidance and supervision are required! Their practice without precise instructions, can become very dangerous.

The first aim of **Pranayama** is to purify the Nadis and gradually control the Prana (vital energy) of the subtle body which moves in our whole system. With this gradual control, the vital energy is made to awake the Kundalini, which will flow in the spinal cord and bring spiritual benefits. However, this practice must be very gradual and regular, following strictly rules and regulations.

Kapalabhati, Bhastrika and **Sitali** are very useful for the awakening of the Kundalini. **Kapalabhati** cleans the skull, the respiratory system, and nasal passages. It cures asthma, develops the lungs, purifies the blood. Owing to its practice, tissues receive a large quantity of oxygen. It tones the circulatory, respiratory, and digestive systems. It is a first step to the practice of Bhastrika pranayama.

Bhastrika means bellows in Sanscrit. Just like the black smith blows the bellows rapidly, one should move one's breath rapidly. It must be Practiced only during the cold season. It increases the gastric fire, destroys phlegm blocking the entrance of the Sushumna Nadi. It breaks the three knots located in the sushumna. It awakens the Kundalini, generates a lot of heat. It removes all diseases arising from excess of Wind, Bile and Phlegm, asthma and destroys impurities and diseases of the nose and chest. It must be learnt from a master.

Sitali pranayama differs entirely from Kapalbhati and Bhastrika. It should be Practiced specially during the hot season as it cools the whole system. The tongue must be folded like a tube and air drawn through it. It purifies blood, quenches thirst, and appeases hunger, it refreshes the whole system. It destroys chronic dyspesia, inflammation of the spleen, skin diseases, fever, indigestion, bilious disorders, poisons, and other diseases.

It cools the brain and brings a lot of peace and happiness. These different kinds of Pranayamas correspond to different stages in the sadhana, only a master can recommend them or forbid them.

The three Yogic seals known as M**ulabandha, Uddiyana bandha**, and **Jalandharbandha** are also very essential in the practice of Kundalini Yoga. They play a major role in channelling energies. The **Mulabandha** is performed by the constriction of the sphincter muscle of the anus. The vital air known as Apana having a downward course is made to move upwards by this constriction. The Apana raised up reaches the region of fire in the navel. There united with Prana, it generates intense heat, which in its turn rouses the Kundalini and makes her enter the Sushumna Nadi in the spine. This seal must be Practiced daily.

Uddiyanabandha must be Practiced after expelling the vital air of the belly. The belly should be contracted and drawn up towards the back. It makes the vital force rise in the Sushumna. It is very good for gastrointestinal disorders. It reduces fat in the belly.

Jalandharbandha must be Practiced after inhalation and the throat must be contracted. This makes the Prana and Apana vital air to unite, directs the vital force to flow in the central canal of the Sushumna. It stops the flow of Vital force in the Ida and Pingala Nadi of the sympathetic chains. It prevents nectar from being absorbed by the gastric fire.

Usually these three seals (bandhas) are automatically performed by the Kundalini after Shaktipat. They accomplish their work for the disciple at the right time without any difficulty. Other mudras which form the very hard and advanced parts of Hatha Yoga are also accomplished naturally by the Kundalini after Shaktipat (Nabho mudra, Shambavi, mudra, Maha Mudra, Yoni mudra, etc...)

These kriyas are very powerful and have very specific actions on the body, and brain, preparing them for higher stages of meditation. All these experiences come as a fruit of the Guru's grace. They are indeed great blessings in spiritual life.

Asanas, Pranayamas, Bandhas, and Mudras, can be

performed separately only if one follows strictly the instructions of a Guru, who knows exactly whether they are compatible with other practices the disciple is already undergoing, like meditation, mantra recitation. Their actions must not be contradictory, or too powerful!

It is of no use to learn a hundred asanas or kriyas needing years and years of practice when a perfect Guru can awake your Kundalini spontaneously and open for you the shortest path leading to self-realization!

(10) THE MANTRA

"At the beginning of time, the Word already was; and God had the Word abiding with him and the word was God. He abodes at the beginning of time with God. It was through him that all things came into being, and without him came nothing that must come to be. In him, there was life and that life was the light of man. And the Word was made flesh and came to dwell among us."

Thus starts the **Holy Gospel** according to **John.**

"God is sound and silence. His name is AUM. At the end of AUM, there is silence. It is a silence of joy. It is the end of the journey where fear and sorrow are no more: steady, motionless, never falling, everlasting, immortal." – Maitri Upanishad.

'AUM, the Eternal, the pure, the awakened, the indeterminate, the flawless, the indescribable that which has neither origin, nor dissolution, the One, The Turiya, that whichever remains One, through the revolutions of the Past, Present and Future, the Always indivisible, the transcending Brahman. From it was born the Parashakti of the essence of Pure Radiant Light.'

- Yoga Chudamani Upanishad

"The Shakti Kundalini, the Coiled One, Luminous, appearing like the fine string of the Lotus stalk; dwells within the Golden Light of the Muladhara. She is the Individual Soul's force and moves in the form of Prana. The great Kundalini is verily the absolute Divine Consciousness, Brahman.

All Letters from A to KSHA are but her forms.

The Great Goddess is the Lord in the Shape of words.'.

- Shiva Samhita.

As the scriptures so beautifully describe, the Lord dwells in Sound and Silence or Silence and Sound. As Static and Dynamic, Shiva, and Shakti, The Father and the Holy spirit. He is so subtle that we can't say where Silence starts and where sound ends. A perfect mingling, yet above all Dual ties, that the Vedas celebrate as "Neti Neti" (neither this nor that).

Only the great Seers in deep contemplation are witnesses to his Glory!

Shabda or Sound is the Adya Spanda, the Primeval Pulsation of the Universe, the cause of the entire creation, a manifestation of Chit Shakti, the power of consciousness whose essence is All Mantras which manifest, themselves in the Ethereal space. Sound or Sabda is further described as Varnatmaka (Lettered sound) and Dhvanyatmaka (unlettered sound). The Dhvani is caused by the striking of two things together, whereas Varna or Anahata is not struck, but self-born.

The entire creation is described as pervaded with Name and Form (Nama, Rupa). Thus Sound is not felt as something heard, it can produce a visual expression, can even be touched. The Manifestations of Sound are further described as, **Para, Pasyanti, Madhyama** and **Vaikhari.**

Para Shabda is unmanifest, it is the causal sound the motionless Kundalini Shakti in the Muladhara Chakra. **Pasyanti** is the first manifested consciousness or Will (Iccha Shakti); sound begins to move as a general motion. Its seat in the Body is from the Muladhara upto the Manipura Chakra. The third aspect of sound is known as Madhyama, it manifests itself in the form of ideas and thoughts, Nama and Rupa. It is produced by the intellect and Jnana Shakti. Its seat goes from the navel up to the heart.

The last aspect **Vaikhari** is the vocal speech (uttered) the expression in the form of words, it is the engendered gross form of sound produced by Kriya Shakti. Its seat is at the throat chakra. Thus, sound evolves from the natural state of undivided and self-born consciousness into its manifestation on the human plane through the intellect and speech.

AUM is the primeval source of sound, The Sphota, the root of all sounds and waves of consciousness, of all Divinities. The undivided consciousness of Brahman (Godhead at the time of creation remultiplies itself into different layers of consciousness which have various functions, represented by the several Seed letters, Divinities, Tattvas. all these are manifestations of the Kundalini. These emanations in the form of seed letters are known as Matrikas, or Beeja Mantras, that are the 52 letters of the Sanskrit alphabet.

They from the Varnamayee aspect of the Kundalini, presided by the different divinities out of which the different elements (tattvas) evolve and work in the different plexuses of the subtle body of the incarnated soul. Each letter represents only an aspect of the deities or certain subtle aspects of the Logos. To reveal the whole form of Divinity, some of those letters must be arranged into a definite sequence of sounds which is known as a Mantra.

'Man' is derived from "Manana' or thinking and "Tra' from 'Trana' or 'Trayate' which means liberation from the bondage of the phenomenal world.

'Manana' is a constant thinking (Brahma chintan), reflection, meditation, which reveal the real understanding of Brahman (supreme divine consciousness) and its creation. A Mantra fulfils (amantrana) the 4 aims of Life called the Chatur Varga: DHARMA (right conduct, religion), ARTHA (wealth), KAMA (desire), MOKSHA (liberation). It frees from fear and finally liberates from the shackles of the World.

Thus, a Mantra is not a mere prayer or formula but a potent sound vibratory force which reveals the form of a Deity and leads to the Highest formless summits of Divine consciousness. The Mantra is the sound body of a Deity which vibrates with Divine consciousness merging into one ness with the Godhead. Mantras are not the property of any religion or faith, we find them in all traditions, known under different names and working through different means. In Hinduism they are usually recorded as VEDIC, PAURANIC and AGAMIC Mantras.

The Vedic Mantras are found in the Vedas and Upanishads,

while The Agamic mantras belong to the various Tantras which form the latest scriptures, also known as the 5th Veda, revealed by Lord Shiva for the benefit of humanity. Here we will just consider these forms of Mantras which are constructive and are spiritual tools for Sadhana.

Certain mantras are also destructive, employed in sorcery, black art and other selfish purposes; they do not enter the spiritual field. The Great Divine Mantras were first perceived by the Seers, who heard them or saw them in their meditation. They recorded them in the form of scriptures or only revealed them through secret initiations. They are surely infinite in number. Mantras are known to have ten parts: Rishi, Chand, Deveta, Bija, Shakti, Kilak, Viniyoga Nyas, Dhyan and Mantra.

'Rishi' refers to the seer who first heard or saw and composed the Mantra. We find in the various scriptures that these mantras are not attributed to one being alone but to several seers who composed them at different times of humanity. "Chand' means the Metre, the form of versification, used to write the mantra. Usually, 7. Metres are employed known as: Gayatri (24), Usnik (28), Anustup (32), Brihati (36), Pankti (40), Tristubh (44), Jagati (48). Each have a certain number of letters; they carry different powers and effects. There are also some submeters, and certain mantras are written in different forms of versification combined.

'Deveta' is the deity one achieves, propitiates, realizes by reciting its corresponding mantras. Several mantras can serve to call the same deity, and are stages in the practice. Here also The Deveta can be the Ishta or chosen deity, representing the ideal of the seeker, or the Kula Deveta, the deity, protecting, and presiding over the family lineage; or a divinity whose help is needed to fulfil certain purposes. The Deveta can assume the form of a God, or Goddess, or Divine couple, like Seeta Ram, Shankar Parvati, or the Formless Paramatma (Oversoul) the Godhead.

'Bija' is the seed letter in the mantra. Each tattva, each deity, has got its bija which empowers the mantra, makes it unfold. It is the root form of the mantra.

'Shakti' is the energy of the mantra. It is represented by a feminine aspect of a goddess or seed letter which imparts power to the mantra. Here also Shakti varies with different mantras. Although the Maha Shakti is the all-Mighty Mother these Shaktis are her multiform emanations.

'Kilak' means support or pillar (keystone). It can be again a seed letter or word of the specific mantra which are supports to the deity.

'Viniyoga': It is the purpose for which one is using the mantra. It can be just to please the deity or achieve the four aims of life, or gain certain powers destroy, control or acquire something. This viniyoga should be stated at the time of making the Sankalpa (mental determination) before the deity.

To each purpose correspond different rules of recitation and worship.

'Nyas' is the placing of the deity on ten different parts of the body. It helps to purify the body allow a better flow of the energies; it grants a quicker perfection of the mantra. These nyas as are also divided into different stages; Rishiyadi Nyas (whole body), Karanyas (fingers), Padanyas) (feet), Hridayadi nyas (heart), Aksharanyas (lettered), Matrikanyas (seedletters), Dignyas (directions). The different parts of the mantra, with its seer, meter, deity, seed mantra etc. are placed on different parts of the body. Then the letters constituting the mantra are also placed on the body. Then seed letters and finally mantras are recited to protect the ten directions all around the worshipper.

'Dhyan' is the meditation required to be done on that particular aspect of the deity, whose grace one is seeking.

And finally, **'Mantra'** refers to the arrangement of the letters constructing the mantra as a whole.

As such a mantra found in any scripture remains a mere verse without life!

The Kularnava Tantra says:

'Only that mantra which is received through the grace of the Guru can give all fulfilment. The realized Guru who is saturated with Divine con sciousness and the vibrations of perfected mantras, instils at the time of Shaktipat his spiritual energy into the mantra; he imparts and awakes its consciousness (chaitanya Shakti). The live mantra now becomes dynamic and directly acts on the awakened Kundalini of the disciple.

As we have already noticed, mantras are infinite in number. We cannot claim that such mantra is better than any other as certain sects do. Each mantra has a different field of action, it corresponds to different needs and fulfils different purposes. On the other hand, apart from finding mantras in the scriptures, they are handed down through different lineages of Gurus, who have attained a perfect practice and knowledge of the means needed for the quick fulfilment and realization of a specific mantra or several mantras.

By receiving the mantra from a perfect Guru, one inherits the benefits and his powers of penance and of his whole lineage which will quickly unfold the latent potency of the mantra and bring quick fulfilment. The same mantra can be practiced differently by different lines of gurus, who achieve their aim by different means. For quick results, one must stick only to the rules prescribed by one's Guru and his lineage.

Mantras are solar or masculine, lunar or feminine and neuter.

The masculine and neuter forms are called Mantra, while the feminine form is known as Vidya.

It is dangerous for anyone to pick up a mantra from scriptures because he likes it and wants to practice it. The mantra must be selected only by the Siddha Guru who knows the needs of the disciple and which form of mantra is most appropriate to his nature and capacities. Following the progress and spiritual evolution of the disciple, the Guru can impart different mantras corresponding to certain stages of sadhana. At the time of initiation two mantras hold the key of the first stages of practice, the Bhoot Shuddi mantra and the Guru mantra, the former has a specific action (purification) while the latter acts more as a whole in the practice. Each mantra is composed by a certain number of letters, which correspond to the meter used to write the mantra. For fulfilment, the mantra must be recited a certain number of times corresponding to the number of its letters. For example, a 10-lettered mantra must be recited 10,00,000 times or more, again all, these rules are revealed by the Guru.

The counted recitation of the mantra is known as Japa which destroys sins, accumulated during several births and finally reveals the Luminous Godhead.

Japa is of three kinds. Vacika or verbal; the mantra is recited aloud; it is the lowest form. Upamshu Japa is done inflow tones, tongues and lips are moved; a slight whisper is only heard. And Manasik Japa, a mental utterance, which is the best form. The mantra must be recited and counted with a rosary (japa mala) made of different material or it can be done while counting on the joints of the fingers (kara japa). 108 times is used as a standard and minimum number of recitations. 100 is considered to be a perfect figure symbolizing the Godhead, and 8 are forms of Maya (illusion or earth, water, fire, air, ether, mind, intellect and ego sense) the individual soul has to cross to regain his true identity. 108 also corresponds to the 54 Sanskrit seed letters (matrikas) recited in order and reverse order. Japa is a very powerful dynamic spiritual force. The recitation must be done carefully with the right pronunciation. The vibratory, effect of Japa on the whole human system is very potent; no mistakes should be made in recitation, or disease might result. Japa which is not counted is known as Asuric Japa (used by the demons). A certain number of rosaries must be recited daily as routine discipline.

The Guru may also ask the disciple to complete the recitation of a certain number of mantras within a definite period of time. For that, prescribed rules are to be observed; this recitation may last for several days, months or years, till the aim of practice is achieved. This process is known as Purascharan or Anusthan.

The rules to be observed vary with mantras and Guru lineage.

Normally if a mantra is a twelve lettered one, one Anusthan to be completed will require the recitation of 12,00,000 mantras; daily recitation will be fixed by the Guru; to it will be added a certain percentage to be dedicated to the manes, brahmans etc. In that way the performance of the Anusthan becomes perfect. The completion of 4 such Anusthans makes a Purascharan. Several purascharan can be performed in a life time; it leads to the perfection of the mantra.

Every year certain periods of days are more auspicious to perform these anusthan (autumn festival dedicated to the Divine Mother) etc...

Eclipse periods are also very fruitful. For the awakening of Kundalini and practice of its Yoga, several mantras and vidyas as are usually known among initiates; still many more are kept secret. The Gayatri mantra, the Navarn mantra, the Shri Vidya mantra, the Kechari mantra, the Kalika mantra, the Hamsah mantra, the Shiva Maha Mantra, the Ram mantra are among the most famous disciplines usually imparted. All these mantras are very potent but correspond to different types and levels of initiates. They reveal different aspects of the Godhead and unfold different forms of Yoga which lead to liberation. The Mantra which is given by the Guru at the time of initiation is known as the Guru mantra. It must be recited during the whole lifetime. It is the bridge between our soul and God.

The Rama mantra holds a prominent place among the Vaishnava scriptures. It is often referred to as Tarak (Saviour mantra which allows the disciple to cross successfully this ocean of mundane existence, attain freedom and liberation. Lord Rama is the seventh incarnation of Vishnu. He represents the very Sattvic aspect of the

Godhead, full of love compassion and mercy. He is the beloved form adored by the great Lord Shiva. The great poet Saint Tulsidas says that Lord Rama as a Divine Incarnation, performed several miracles and accomplished wonderful tasks, but it is still nothing compared to his name who saved millions of souls from the raging fire of the world.

The poet writes: 'I greet the name of Rama, chief of the Raghu's, composed of seed letters, representing the Fire god, the Sun god and the Moon god (Ra a ma). It is the same as Brahma (the creative aspect of God), Vishnu (his preserving aspect) and Shiva (destructive aspect) and the vital breath of the Vedas. It is unqualified, peerless and a mine of virtues. It is the great spell which Lord Shiva mutters in Kashi (Benares) and, where imparted, leads to emancipation."

The name of Rama is the wish yielding tree, the very home of beatitude in Kali Yuga, the reward of all virtuous acts, say the Vedas, seers, and Puranas. Through the repetition of Rama's name, the ocean of Mundane existence itself gets dried up."

Ra is the Agni matra (seed letter of fire), it is the heating, consuming factor, the root of all modifications and decay.

A is all pervading.

M is the sustaining principle (soma matra), the essence of life, immortal, the divine nectar.

These two principles are at the root of creation, preservation, and destruction.

R (visarga) heats excites, while M (anusvara) soothes. Agni corresponds to Nada and Soma to Bindu.

Ra is in the Manipura chakra while M is in the mahayoni of the

Sahasrar chakra. When these seed letters unite in the Sahasrar, supreme bliss is gained, this union is purely sattvik and leads to the highest Yoga.

"One day Shri Ramkrishna initiated Narendra with the name of Rama; it produced a miraculous effect. Narendra (Swami Vivekananda) was filled with bliss and intoxicated, went round and round the house uttering the name of Rama He was in such exalted mood that none dared approach him. It took several hours before Narendra regained normal consciousness."

The name of Rama is no other than AUM. It is a great bestower of Devotion, strength, knowledge, bliss, joy, love and peace. It grants all virtues and destroys all sin. It is the great saviour in this dark age of Kali. Lord Hanuman had attained such a perfection of the Ram mantra that he could even control and challenge Lord Rama himself.

Mantra Japa serves as a bridge between the individual soul and the Lord. Mantra Japa and meditation are surely the best spiritual tools leading to liberation. Mantra recitation should not be underestimated by the ignorant.

If practiced with due concentration, faith, devotion, and right pronunciation it grants high results. The mantra must be duly awakened by the Siddha Guru at the time of initiation. Its dynamic force will automatically start to act on the physical and mental being of the disciple.

Its first effect will be felt on the movement of breath. It will gradually balance the rhythm of inhalation and exhalation and the two vital airs, Prana and Apana. The rhythm of breath will gradually decrease, the vital force quiet down, turning the mind within.

The vital force which flows usually in the Ida and Pingala Nadis (sides of the spine) will be made to flow by the power of the mantra through the central duct Sushumna, awakening the Kundalini.

In short Mantra japa acts as a natural pranayama and spontaneous awakener of the Divine within.

By this direct action on the physical body, mantra japa removes impurities in the system, cures diseases, brings balance into all the vital functions.

The Nadis are cleared up, the vital force is toned up and flows with more vigour.

The whole body is strengthened.

The power of the Mantra leads to a balanced motion of Prana, which brings peace in the mind; thoughts decrease, the subconscious mind gets purified, evil habits are removed. With practice the mantra works throughout the day; even at night it continues to be recited automatically.

After regulating the movement of breath, the mantra brings Pratyahara or restraint of the senses from their objects; the senses are turned inwardly and more detachment is achieved. From that Dharana is gained, the mind becomes concentrated, clearer, more and more focussed on the Lord. Finally, the Mantra leads to spontaneous Dhyan or meditation, which soon becomes Samadhi. The Mantra, its Deity and the worshipper must become one. This is the aim of Sadhana. Of course, the progression of mantra sadhana must go through stages. A constant and regular practice is required.

The recitation of the mantra brings all kinds of spiritual experiences: hearing of divine sounds, visualization of the deity, the guru, gods, siddhas etc. It gradually develops psychic powers; telepathy, clairvoyance, etc. The effect of the Mantra is not only felt within but also all around the Upasak. The whole atmosphere vibrates with mantra; every object around is permeated by Mantra Shakti. The abodes of great Mantra Siddhas are so charged with mantra shakti that we can even hear the mantra as soon as we enter their ashram; or experience a spontaneous spiritual awakening, automatic meditation. Trees, birds even stones vibrate with the divine name.

The Mantra is the Guru, the Kundalini Herself which unfolds step by step the different aspects of yoga needed for perfection. It first acts as Hatha Yoga by regulating the breaths, allowing a natural Pranayam.

As Raja yoga it leads to concentration, meditation and samadhi.

As Bhakti Yoga it awakens love for God, devotion, and surrender.

As Karma Yoga it grants a lot of energy and inspiration to do good just for the sake of goodness. The Mahatma Gandhi was a great Mantra Upasaka.

As Jnana Yoga it destroys dualities, the ego sense and grants the highest knowledge of the Self.

As Laya Yoga it dissolves the mind into the Anahata sounds.

Thus all mantras are forms of the Divine Kundalini Shakti, the Mother of All Yogas Lord Shiva says in the Maha Nirvana Tantra:

"Thou art the Adya Parama Shakti, the supreme prior dial Shakti. Thou art all power. Endless and of varied color and form, are thy appearances and various are the strenuous efforts whereby the worshippers may realize them."

"Thou art both subtle and gross, manifested and veiled, formless yet with form."

(11) THE YANTRA

The mantra is the sound body of the deity, to which correspond one or several yantras. The Yantra is a diagram embossed on metal or drawn on paper or other material. It is the form pattern of the particular deity. The different triangles, figures, and lotuses represent the different aspects of the divine. Yantra means free from all fear, and saviour. After the due ceremony, the life force of the devata is infused into the diagram which becomes a live source of energy, bliss, protection, and blessings, absorbing the divine like the pores of the skin, invisibly. The Yantra represents the outer form of worship that can be accomplished inwardly by advanced yogis.

All the mantras and aspects of the divine are found in the different plexuses of the subtle body. This inner form of worship leads to the highest summits of meditation, as Lord Shankaracharya writes in the Saundarya Lahari:

"Great Ones experience the supreme wave of bliss, viewing in their minds cleansed of dirt and ignorance the facet of your form, resplendent like lightning, existing in the sun, moon and fire as also in the six psychic centres, but above all shining in the thousand-petalled lotus." V., 21.

(12) DHYAN OR MEDITATION

Up till now, we have seen how the observance of Yamas, Niyamas, Asanas, pranayamas Mantra Japa form several limbs in the practice of Kundalini Yoga. Those are the stages that finally lead to the highest states of Dhyan and Samadhi. The term Meditation encompasses Dhyan and Samadhi, beginning with concentration and reaching total merging into Divine consciousness. In the Yoga Sutras, Patanjali Muni says: "Dhyan or Meditation, is the uninterrupted flow of consciousness towards the object of concentration."

"When the form of the object of concentration even disappears, it becomes Samadhi."

Dhyan and Samadhi are the last stages by which the disciple merges into Divine Awareness. The individual soul finally returns to its source, all dualities vanish.

The Dhyan Bindu Upanishad says:

"Even if sins accumulated through thousands of previous births assume a mountain like form extending over an area of several leagues, it can be cloven through and shattered to pieces by Dhyan Yoga, Meditation on Brahman; it is the only means."

Now how should one proceed with the practice of Meditation?

Like the other limbs of Yoga, it comprises several stages and responds to varied forms of practice.

A firm and peaceful posture (asana) is the first requirement. If your body aches, your limbs cannot remain in the same position for a long while, and it will be extremely difficult to concentrate the mind and direct it towards meditation.

For that purpose, we have to practice a posture in which we feel comfortable and at ease. The trunk must be kept erect, along with the neck and head. The head and spine should be in a straight line. This will help the energies to flow freely and the Kundalini will be easily awakened.

To avoid any distractions and focus the senses within, a quiet undisturbed place should be chosen. We must sit daily at the same time at the same place and keep this habit regular which will generate increasing energy and protection.

Early mornings and evenings are the auspicious peaceful times for meditation when night vanishes into daytime and dusk into darkness.

To bring a quicker and better concentration, Mantra Japa should be performed before meditation; it purifies the mind, concentrates the energies, regulates the movement of breath, it leads to spontaneous states of meditation. This combination of Japa and Dhyan is very useful and powerful. All the energy, accumulated through Mantra Japa will serve as dynamic support for meditation. A kind of spiritual fuel. Various forms of concentration and meditation are described in the scriptures. Surely the easiest and most natural way is to concentrate on the movement of one's breath, it is extremely subtle and the closest to us, it leads to quick spontaneous meditation.

With eyes closed we should concentrate on the space between the eyebrows, known as the third eye. Along with it take 25 to 50 deep equal breaths through the nose only, then resume normal breathing and observe the movement of inspiration and expiration. When you inhale you can recite mentally Ram or Om. Watch the vital air entering the nose and going down to the umbilicus and when you exhale count 1, 2, 3 etc.

By this joining of the Divine name and counting, the mind will quickly concentrate and loose itself into the movement of breath, which is the motion of Prana (life force) of the incarnated soul (Hamsa). The scripture say that we are unconsciously repeating daily the SO HAM HAM SAH mantra known as the Ajapa Gayatri 21 600 times combined with the natural movement of inhalation and exhalation. The process of joining the name of Ram or Om with counting is similar to this Ajapa Gayatri.

However, it must be kept in mind, that this process is only the very first step towards meditation, but should not be neglected; it will gradually lead the mind into higher levels of concentration. As long as concentration and spontaneous meditation are not achieved, this process will be very useful. It will regulate the Prana and direct the Kundalini through the central Sushumna Nadi in the spine.

In the beginning of practice several experiences are common to all seekers. The body aches, the mind becomes all of a sudden active; thoughts rush by hundreds of negative feelings spring up; sometimes sleep comes or hyper nervousness. The sudden search for concentration seems to revolt the whole being. Understand, it is just a momentary experience. When you want to clear a pond the whole water becomes dark and muddy, fishes move here and there, the water weeds float all around. It becomes very hard to know where the pure water has gone. Similar is the state of mind of the beginner, very agitated and veiled! This process of meditation is just a technique yogic kriya needed to achieve concentration.

What we require to go ahead is self-surrender We must open ourselves to the grace and influence of the Divine power working through the Guru Meditation is not something we can build up by our efforts, intelligence, reflexions, wishes. No, it is beyond the reach of ordinary judgement and logic. It is the hidden property of the perfected ones, who alone have the capacity to unfold the art of natural and spontaneous meditation. This science of meditation is known only to the realized ones; Meditation is a form of their grace.

Guru Gita says: "The essence of Meditation is the form of the Guru. The essence of Liberation is the grace of the Guru."

Shaktipat has established for the disciple the link with Grace and the lineage of the Gurus. Now we must open ourselves to their guidance and action working through the inner Kundalini Shakti, the living form of grace, the Great Mother of Yoga. No need to try to jump over the stages, it is of no avail. The Kundalini alone must be allowed to perform her work. The more you take care to observe the preliminary steps of Yoga (yama niyama etc.) the more the shakti will be helped in her work!

As soon as you sit for meditation, you will feel the Kundalini awakening, she will purify your body, clean your mind. Do not try to control or stop whatever happens to you. She has complete awareness of your needs. Let all the kriyas happen freely in your body, do not worry about your restless mind! All these reactions are prompted by the purifying divine force. She will have to remodel. transform your whole being. It will take time, be patient!

Let your progress follow its natural course, do not interfere. Be regular in your practice always. Keep your mind busy with the recitation of the Mantra, it will gradually annihilate thoughts. If you feel like falling asleep during Meditation or lying down let it happen, it will help you to enter a state called Tandra; it is not an ordinary sleep, it is a meditative state, a kind of trance that will make you travel to different realms, various worlds unknown to your waking consciousness. You will meet strange beings, Gods, Goddesses, Siddhas. Your astral body will leave your body very easily, giving you a great feeling of freedom, open for you new dimensions of consciousness. Your Guru may also appear before you in meditation or in dreams, to give you precise instructions to improve your practice. You will derive great delight while meditating upon his divine radiant form.

All these experiences may appear a bit anarchist in their manifestations; do not worry, they have definite purposes. With time you will feel that you have no more difficulty in concentrating, the movement of thoughts has slowed down a great deal, and you enter automatically the Tandra state, losing your body consciousness. When meditation gets over, you feel very light, peaceful, and energetic. All the negativities which were springing out of the mind have subsided and given place to peaceful and loving feelings.

Your consciousness is no more limited as before, you experience yourself constantly linked with a higher power, even during waking hours. The Divine Shakti helps you in your daily tasks, everything becomes more spontaneous. You may hear different sounds, see brilliant lights, and at times contemplate the chakras opening in your subtle body. At times you may get frightful experiences and horrible dreams; you may feel you are going through the experience of death, see your own body lifeless, etc

All these experiences vary with disciples. Some people do not get any of those they just experience peace and joy. Experiences are encouraging signs; they must not be mistaken for divine realizations. The spiritual path is very long and tortuous. A few months of practice cannot be of much avail. A whole lifetime is needed. And for that, we will have to overcome many obstacles coming during practice. At every stage, progress must be conquered against great resistance.

DANGERS

It is indeed very hard to harmonize spiritual life with the vibrations of the world. Several hostile forces wish to utilize our lower nature and pervert it. It is an absolute necessity to keep ourselves constantly awake and vigilant and stick to our central will guided by divine Truth. We must step back and remain a witness to whatever happens to us and refuse to answer the many calls of the outer world. Maha Rishi Patanjali enumerates these obstructing, distractions: "Disease, dullness, doubt, lack of enthusiasm, lethargy clinging to sense enjoyments, false perception, inability to find a firm ground for spiritual investigation, unsteadiness of mind resulting in failure, sorrowful mood, psychological despair." All these obstacles correspond to these parts of our being, which have not been tamed yet.

We should not get depressed at the sight of our defects, wrong attitudes, or failures. Spiritual life is always made up of ups and downs. We need to be patient and develop a state of detachment, peace, and equanimity. We have to understand that lust, desires, pride, dullness are only wrong movements of our lower nature, they have nothing to do with reality; we have to learn to transform them, and transcend them. And meditation greatly helps in that task.

The Guru who keeps a constant astral link with us knows inwardly our difficulties and through his willpower removes several of these obstacles or gives us the means to overcome them. Like birds feeding and training their young ones, he will have to set and build up the spiritual frame within us, trace the path of practice, correct our mistakes, and give us hope, faith and encouraging experiences. In the beginning of practice his action will be more direct and sensible, till the disciple reaches higher levels, then he will allow the young ones to leave their nest, keeping an eye over their progression.

Self-effort and grace must work jointly, they need each other at all stages of progress; the disciple will have to avoid evil company, too much mixing with people, strong attachment to family, wealth etc. Overeating, over-fasting, overworking, physical activities need to be balanced. Acquisition of psychic powers, spiritual pride, wrong interpretations given to lower states of Samadhi, must be checked. Humility must stand as a good referee. To overcome drawbacks a constant practice of Japa, anusthan, upasana, dhyan, will surely fashion the inner Guru, the divinity within.

A very significant form of meditation is given by Maharishi Patanjali in his Yoga Aphorisms to eliminate mental distractions, obstacles and allow a higher progress for the disciple.

"Or meditating on the heart, consciousness of one who has

given up all attachments, to sense objects, free from conditioning.' V. 37.

It is a matter of experience that the company of great saints or one's Guru is elevating and peace-giving. Meditation on their divine form, and divine qualities, quickly stabilize the mind. The Body of the Guru is not an ordinary body of flesh; he is saturated with divine consciousness and encompasses all the aspects of divinity.

Its mere remembrance infuses peace and strengthening vibrations into the disciple's astral body. In that way, the power given at the time of Shaktipat can be constantly rejuvenated. Meditation on the Guru's form gradually leads the disciple to identification with the Guru principle. Merging into the Guru's form opens the doors of the formless. This explains why most religions revere and worship one physical form or another of the divine.

Lord Rama after receiving the final Shaktipat from his Guru Vasistha, reached the transcendental realms, and, regaining body consciousness declared:

"There is nothing superior to self-knowledge, nothing superior to the Guru."

Narada Muni in his Bhakti Sutras supports these views:

"Higher spiritual realization in the form of Para Bhakti (supreme devotion) Samadhi; is attainable by the grace of God and Godmen alone."

"But it is extremely difficult to come into contact with a great soul and to be benefited by his company; the influence of such a one is subtle, incomprehensible and unerringly infallible in its effect."

He adds further:

"Evil company, however, is fit only to be shunned by all means. For it leads to the rousing up of desire, anger, delusion, loss of memory, loss of discrimination and utter ruin in the end."

Spiritual life has constantly to find its way between divine and evil forces. It requires time and practice to discriminate between the two. The great realized ones proclaim that this fight ends only when the Highest goal is reached. Before that a complete transformation of the physical, vital, and mental bodies must take place. Very subtle chemical changes happen in the brain, the nervous system. All the cells of the body must be transformed through meditation and Mantra Shakti. It is a very long patient process taking years of intense practice and concentration on the divine aim.

Through, feelings, emotions, perceptions, opinions, reactions have to be given a new turn and be reshaped by the power of the inner life. What a conquest it is against the automatic dull movements of nature.

How could we succeed without divine help?

We find in the Vedas that the seers were constantly asking and praying for divine help and support.

"We invoke the resplendent and adorable Lord, the preserver of the spiritual fire of devotees. May he be with us hither to awaken divine consciousness and happiness.

May the Lord render the fiends powerless and make sterile the devourers of the virtuous."

"Awaken the pair of mental and vital powers, yoke them every morning in work and worship." Rg V. 1.22.

Innumerable such hymns were composed and addressed to

the multiforme manifestations of the Godhead as if a man without Grace could no longer live and evolve. What a magnificent example of self-surrender and devotion it gives!

(13) MIND SOURCE OF BONDAGE AND LIBERATION

The more meditation deepens and intensifies the more subtle perceptions, and realizations become. The seeker undergoes a gradual purification of the five sheaths along with emancipation from their binding elements.

The Maitri Upanishad says:

"Mind is indeed the source of bondage and the source of liberation. To be bound to things of this world: this is bondage. To be free from them: this is liberation."

Mind is often designated as 'Avidya' or Ignorance. Unless it is purified and freed from false identifications, no self-awareness can be felt.

It is said: 'Identification with the body (annamaya kosha) is the root that produces the misery of birth.' It is born of semen and ovum, which are nothing but the transformation of food. It has to undergo the six modifications (shad bhava vikarars) (existence, birth, growth, change, decay and death). As such it is permanently under the spell of the mind and the outer world.

The subtle body and the causal body are verily the root and cause of this ignorance. The five vital airs (prana, apana, udana, samana, vyana) and the five organs of action (vak, speech), Pani (organ of grasping), Pada (organ of locomotion), Upastha (organ of generation), Payu (organ of excretion) form together the vital part (pranamaya kosha) of the subtle body. Apart from complete dependence on the mind, it constantly receives impulses and vibrations from the different universal vital forces.

The mental sheath of the subtle body (manomaya kosha) composed of the five organs of knowledge: Shrotra (sense of hearing), Tvak (sense of touch), Chakshu (sense of sight), Jihva (sense of taste), Ghrana (sense of smell), Manas (thinking and doubting the conscious mind), Chitta (subconscious mind, memorizing) act directly on the vital and physical sheath. fed with numerous desires and deluding influences of the universal subconscious mind, cause diversity and unsteadiness. When the five organs of knowledge are associated with Buddhi (intellector determinative faculty) and Ahamkara (ego sens). They form the Vijnana- maya kosha or knowledge sheath of the subtle body.

The intellect and ego-sense are limited, they influence the performance of good and evil actions, and experience their results. They act as the most subtle veil creating the illusory perception of reality, or the finest instruments of Ignorance.

Ignorance (Ajnana), Avidya is referred to as the causal body, cause of the other two bodies and the blissful sheath (anandamaya kosha), the experience of pleasure associated with Priya (joy), Moda (delight), Pramoda (bliss of enjoyment).

In short, 'Mind' is that ignorant cause working through the four principles known as Manas, Buddhi, Chitta, Ahamkara called the

Antahkarana (inner instrument). The highest part of meditation and spiritual practices aim at crossing and transcending this false perception brought about by the Antahkarana.

In the Viveka Chudamani, Shri Shankara writes:

"The truth of the Paramatman is extremely subtle and cannot be reached by the gross outgoing tendency of the mind. It is only accessible to noble souls with perfectly pure minds, using Samadhi brought by an extraordinary fineness of the mental state. As gold purified by thorough heating on the fire gives up its impurities and attains to its lustre, so the mind through meditation gives up its impurities and attains to the reality of Brahman.

By Samadhi all desires are destroyed and lead directly to the realization of the bliss of Brahman; The One without a second.' V. 360.

"This bondage can be destroyed neither by weapons nor by wind, nor by fire, nor by millions of acts; by nothing except the wonderful sword of knowledge that comes of discrimination, sharpened by the grace of the Lord.' V. 147.

(14) REACHING THE GOAL

In his Yoga Darshanam, Patanjali Muni at once describes the aim and the means of evolution:

"Yogah chitta vritti nirodah.' "Yoga is restraining the mind stuff (chitta) from taking various forms 'vrittis'."

Now what is 'chitta' and what are the 'vrittis'?

"Chitta' is often translated as mind stuff or subconscious mind; the 'vrittis' are the mental modifications taking the forms of moods, feelings, attractions, aversions Like all the other planes of consciousness, the sub conscient has two forms: one universal and the other individual. It stands in between the conscient and the inconscient. Whatever we experience, good or bad during our day-to-day life gets stored up in the sub-conscient. It contains all the primitive reactions of life, in a kind of fluid form, which gradually develop into a part of our consciousness. All our samskaras (prenatal tendencies), vasanas (subtle desires) accumulated during several lifetimes also remain there in a seed form.

This Chitta is a kind of huge storehouse that records all the movements of our physical, vital and mental beings. The subconscious has three motions, receiving (in going) keeping and outgoing. Whatever we experience in contact with the outer world through the medium of the senses, gets immediately recorded and a lot of experiences rejected by our consciousness take refuge there too. Certain of these impressions stored up, soon come back on the surface, creating a constant repetition through the movements of thoughts, dreams and stand at the root of our habits, instincts, memories, features of character.

Thus, the Chitta remains constantly under the spell of fluctuations, repetitions and mental turmoil called the 'vrittis'; which prevent mind from quietude and stability.

The Vedanta Philosophy enumerates mental modifications as such: Raga (sexual pleasure), Dvesha (hatred), Kama (desire), Krodha (anger), Lobha (miserliness), Moha (infatuation), Mada (pride), Matsarya (jealousy), Irshya (intolerance), Asuya (envy), Dambha (ostentation for name and fame), Darpa (arrogance), Ahamkara (egoism), Iccha (action of necessity), Bhakti (devotion), Shraddha (faith).

Most of those modifications are negative by nature, only the last two have a spiritual potency, they stand as the keystone of evolution. The practice of Yoga aims to purify these lower mental modifications, lessen their development into a definite form of character, habits but also to stop the incoming of further negative impressions into the Subcon scient which would create new seeds.

This last stage of the practice is only obtained when purity has destroyed all negativities and conditioning, raising the consciousness to its highest level which at once suppresses the formation of new impressions and seeds, by the intensity of its divine vibrations. It leaves nothing, and the soul is manifested just as it is, in its own glory. Patanjali calls this state: "the seedless Nirbija Samadhi."

In other words, it becomes total self-awareness or Aparoksanubhuti. The culmination and summit of all spiritual practices. All the binding tendencies of the mind stuff working through the intellect and ego are destroyed. It is the cessation of all mental activities at all levels, which leads to a super consciousness, supramental state, the Asamprajnata or Nirvikalpa Samadhi.

The Yogi is said to have attained the realization of complete freedom and isolation 'Kaivalya', the uninterrupted pure self-awareness, called the 'Dharma Megha', the cloud of virtue. The Kundalini Shakti remains united with her Lord in the Sahasrar Padma enjoying supreme bliss.

The Hamsopanishad says:

'Wherefore, when the mind is dissolved in the Mind, when volition and misconception are lost when virtue and vice have been burnt in the fire of superior knowledge, then Sada-shiva the great Lord, who is of the character of Energy, Shakti inhering in all things, who has established himself as Sat (existence), Chit (consciousness) and Ananda (bliss) in the entire phenomenal world. Who is self-effulgent, immaculate, sentient, eternal, non-attached, and superlatively peaceful causes himself to shine as without a counterpart.'

"There the sun shines not, nor the moon, nor the stars, lightning shine not there and much less earthly fire. From his light all these give light and his radiance illumines all creation. Only the wise who see him in their souls attain to peace eternal.'

– Katha Upanishad.

"The wise and true seekers realize God through transcendental meditation within their self. They see him vividly as the eye ranges over the sky." - Rig Veda.

"Having attained the Guru as his helmsman and made a boat of his subtle teachings by dint of the impressions left on their minds during their tutelage, thus wise men cross the ocean of worldly existence.". –Kundalini Upanishad.

"Sometimes a fool, sometimes a sage, sometimes possessed of regal splendour, sometimes wandering, sometimes behaving like a motionless python, sometimes wearing benignant expression, sometimes honoured, sometimes insulted, sometimes unknown; thus lives the man of realization, ever happy with supreme bliss." - Viveka

Chudamani V.542.

Having attained the Goal, certain Yogis come down from the highest Nirvikalpa Samadhi to a state known as Sahaja Samadhi (natural Samadhi), divine state, through which they can work for the good of humanity and become Teachers of men.

(15) QUESTIONS

Pondering over the intricacies of Spiritual life and the High Practices of Yoga, some questions readily come to Mind.

Are all eligible for such practices? or is it the only concealed property of renunciates, monks and mystics?

Can householders be admitted to climb such steps?

Is the western trained mind capable to grasp and digest such precepts?

We could first answer here by asking another question:

Have all human beings a right to education, Peace and happiness? Certainly yes; but all have not got the same immediate needs, capacities, abilities to acquire them.

We live in a world where all kinds of souls run along, sometimes separated by several lifetimes of evolution; but still they all look like each other: human beings !

The Seers clearly felt the importance to establish grades in the spiritual sciences, which would enable all at a point or another of evolution to enter on the path. No less than the great Lord Shiva himself, visualizing the effects the Dark Iron Age (Kali Yuga) was having upon humanity, started imparting the great teachings of the Tantras which are in no way different from the ancient Vedic Lore, just more adapted to the present time.

These Tantras describe three kinds of temperaments, characters (Bhava) corresponding to the inherent dispositions of different classes of men. The Pasubhava (animal type), the Virabhava (heroic type) and the Divyabhava (divine type).

The 'Pashu' is the kind of human being in whom the qualities of inertia (tamas) preponderate. He lives an ignorant life; lacking faith, discrimination, rules, and regulations. He thinks himself to be only a body and lives accordingly, concerned mainly by food and sensual satisfaction. He revolves like a blind man bound to the wheel of the world. The Vira' has developed his intellect to a higher level and can discriminate Good from Evil; but his character remains highly influenced by Rajas (activity) and Ego-sense. He requires such kinds of practice challenging his active sensual nature.

The 'Divya' has already developed higher spiritual qualities in previous lives. His character is dominated by Sattva (purity), peace, devotion, discrimination, divine features. As such these three kinds of characters can be found at all levels of society. All can be benefited by spiritual practices provided they follow the prescribed means allotted to them. Thus the lowest type being able to climb to the highest through self-effort, grace and practice!

Now all have got a common point, they all need to be guided by a master who will reveal to them their respective duties and forms of practices, different for householders and renunciates. It does not mean to say, that some are higher than others. No! They must go through different experiences of life, tests, and difficulties. If they follow strictly and successfully the teachings imparted to them, they are all supposed to reach a common goal!

To illustrate this, there is a beautiful story related by the great Swami Vivekananda: "A young Sannyasin went to a forest; there he meditated, worshipped, and practiced Yoga for a long time. After years of hard work and Practice, he was one day sitting under a tree when some dry leaves fell upon his head. He looked up and saw a crow and a crane fighting on the top of the tree, which made him very angry. He said, 'What'! Dare you throw these dry leaves upon my head! As with these words he angrily glanced at them, a flash of fire went out. Such was the Yogi's power and burnt the birds to ashes. He was very glad, almost overjoyed at this development of power; he could burn the crow and the crane by a look!

After a while he had to go to the town to beg for his bread. He went, stood at a door and said "Mother, give me food!'

A voice came from inside the house, "Wait a little my son!'

The young man thought: 'You wretched woman, how dare you make me wait! You do not know my power!

While he was thinking thus the voice came again: 'Boy, don't be thinking too much of yourself. Here is neither crow nor crane!

He was astonished. Still, he had to wait. At last the woman came, and he fell at her feet and said: "Mother, how did you know that ?'

She said: "My boy, I do not know your Yoga or your practices. I am a common simple woman. I made you wait because my husband is ill and I was nursing him. All my life I have struggled to do my duty.

When I was unmarried, I did my duty to my parents; now that I am married, I do my duty to my husband. That is all the Yoga I Practice. But by doing my duty I have become illuminated; thus, I could read your thoughts and know what you had done in the forest. If you want to know something higher than this, go to the market of such and such a town where you will find, a butcher (lowest class of people in India), who will tell you something that you will be very glad to learn!

The sanyasin thought, why should I go to that town and to this butcher! But after what he had seen, his mind opened a little, so he went. When he came near the town, he found the market, and there he saw, at a distance, a big fat butcher cutting meat with big knives, talking, and bargaining with different people. The young man said: 'Lord help me! Is this the man from whom I am going to learn? He is the incarnation of a demon, if he is anything.' In the meantime, the man looked up and said:

'O Swami did that Lady send you here? Take a seat until I have done my business! 'The Sannyasin thought: 'What comes to me here? He took his seat. The man went on with his work and after he had finished he took his money and said to the sannyasin: 'Come, sir, come to my home!! On reaching home the butcher gave him a seat, saying, 'Wait here and went into the house. He then bathed his old father and mother, fed them and did all he could to please them, after which he came to the sannyasin and said, "Now sir you have come here to see me. What can I do for you?' The Sannyasin asked him a few questions about soul and about God, and the butcher gave him a lecture which forms a part of the Mahabharata. It contains one of the highest flights of the Vedanta.

When the butcher finished his teaching, the sannyasin felt astonished. He said: "Why are you in that body? With such a knowledge as yours why are you in a butcher's body and doing such filthy, ugly work?"

"My son", replied the butcher, "no duty is ugly, no duty is impure. My birth placed me in these circumstances and this environment. In my boyhood I learned the trade. I am unattached and try to do my duty well. I try to do my duty as a householder and try to do all I can to make my father and mother happy. I neither know your Yoga, nor have I become a sannyasin, nor did I go out of the world into a forest. Nevertheless, all that you have heard and seen has come to me through the unattached doing of my duty which belongs to my position."

Which does not mean to say that all butchers become realized beings. Great Sannyasins can be found among renunciates, realized women among housewives, divine knowledge gifted people among hard workers.

Now, can westerners follow the path of Yoga?

Why not! They are westerners only by name! Who knows who they were in previous birth! Rather, is the western society able to grasp the teachings of Yoga and capable to digest its uplifting precepts.

A lot of attempts are going on all over the world now, it is too early to draw any conclusion about results or failures recorded. The teachings of Yoga and Vedanta are surely universal in theory, three things are essential for their success: great realized Masters, a surrounding adapted for their growth, and real genuine people to Practice them. The surroundings of an Ashram, and the physical presence of the Master are essential in the beginning of practice. They will serve as channels for a life built upon discipline and self-surrender.

A vast difference has to be made between what we read about spirituality, the philosophies creating high intellectual speculation and the routine practices with their rites, customs, rules, regulations, repetitions, obstacles. In fact, very few become qualified to walk on the summits of Vedanta! The trainings given by a great Guru are very essential in all forms of practice from Hatha Yoga to Vedanta. The western mind, accustomed to pick up things here and there, will surely suffer from the uniformity of spiritual life, which very often goes beyond standard understanding and so-called logic! Self-surrender, meditation, devotion is rather terms alien to the average western man. Here everything must be learned anew, not through the intellect, but through the heart, through intuition and direct experience. It requires a lot of patience, tolerance, faith, and training. A lot of changes will have to occur, sometimes hard and painful but if we stick to our aim major transformation will be the reward.

Untimely attempts to search for independence, to adapt the teachings to one's liking, and even transform them into a Western labelled product are very dangerous and will lead nowhere at all.

Meditation, Yoga, Vedanta belong to the East, to the very ancient traditions of India. Refusing to respect them, to understand them and adapt oneself to them cannot be of any value. The use made of Eastern teachings as fashions is equally hopeless. Eastern traditions are masters in possessing precepts and techniques aiming at uprooting man's ignorance, the dark shackles of heredity and civilization. Universality must become the reward!

Although the Ashram is to serve as a dynamic training centre, its high spiritual vibrations act as a strong protecting Armor, completely immune and cut from the outer world. The great difficulty often met in the western world, is into preserving and maintaining the high standards of spiritual vibrations and benefits in the day-to-day rhythms of worldly life. How can one transform one's own everyday life, with its specific physical and emotional limitations, into a more positive and divine evolutionary background? This evolution is a step to be taken by all and as self-efforts cannot alone remove.

Great saints like Swami Vivekananda, Swami Ram Tirth, Paramhansa Yogananda and others made the decisive step to adapt themselves outwardly to western standards in order to deliver their teachings. They were the pioneers who started establishing a bridge between East and West, the harbingers of Man's Universality.

Thanks to their blessings, the seeds of spirituality grew in abundance in the West and they continue to develop all over the world, The silent effect of Divine vibrations generated by Great saints and meditators, the power of peace, love, brotherhood are surely the tools of Man's evolution. Mankind can only progress through a change of consciousness, it must start individually and gradually reach each and every heart for common upliftment!

"The idea of man is to see God in everything. But if you cannot see Him in everything, see Him in one thing in that thing which you like the best and then see Him in another. So, on you can go, there is an infinite life before the soul. Take your time and you will achieve your end.' - Swami Vivekananda.

"The generalization of Yoga in humanity must be the last victory of Nature over her delays and concealments. Even as now by the progressive mind in science she seeks to make all mankind fit for the dull development of the mental life, so by Yoga must she inevitably seek to make all mankind fit for the higher evolution, the second birth, the spiritual existence.

"And as the mental life uses and perfects the material, so will the spiritual use and perfect the material and the mental existence as the instruments of a divine self-expression."

"Our liberation and perfection is to transcend ignorance, bondage and weakness and live in him in relation to the world and nature with the divine power freedom and self-knowledge."

"For it is God alone, by the possession of the Divine only that all the discords of life can be resolved, and therefore the raising of men towards the Divine is in the end the one effective way of helping mankind." - Shri Aurobindo.

(16) THE HASTAMAMALAKA STOTRA
(Shri Shankaracharya)

To end here this work, we have chosen a beautiful Vedantic prayer, a poem written by the Great Adya Shankaracharya, who so harmoniously combined the features of a Siddha Yogi, a philosopher, a poet and a seer. This poem came to life when Shri Shankara met a young boy, called Hastamalaka who looked quite indifferent to all worldly life. His behaviour resembled that of a dumb and deaf man. He was a constant source of worry for his family as he refused to study and learn the enjoined duties of his Brahmin lineage; he would hardly partake food offered to him and play with other children.

None knew what was wrong with him. Despite his strange behaviour, he always looked happy, cheerful at peace. When Shri Shankara arrived in the village of Shreebali, South India, the child's father described his son's condition to the sage and prayed for help.

Shri Shankara immediately recognized the child to be a born Siddha (perfect one) whose behaviour can only be found in highly spiritual evolved beings. Out of love and joy at the sight of the illumined boy, Shri Shankara addressed his future disciple thus;

THE HASTAMAMALAKA STOTRA

Shri Shankara queried:

Beloved child! Who are you? Whose son, are you? What is your name? Where do you come from? Where are you going?

For my good please answer my questions. You are so dear to

me.

Hastamalaka replied: I am neither a man nor a god, nor a demi god; neither a priest, nor a warrior, nor a trader nor a low caste.

I am neither a celibate, nor a householder, nor a hermit nor a mendicant, I am verily the Eternal Self Gnosis.

I am the Soul Supreme, the embodied Eternal Knowledge Divine freed from the last barriers of space, acting at the root of mind and senses' activity; like the sun impels people to perform their duties.

I am the Soul Supreme, the embodied Eternal Self Gnosis, whose essence is pure consciousness, like the fire is heat, which sustains the gross mind and induces the senses to perform their respective functions.

I am the Soul Supreme, the embodied Self Knowledge Divine. As the reflection of the face in a mirror is only the face itself, so the individual Soul is only the Supreme reflected in the Intellect.

I am the Soul Supreme, the embodied Eternal Seif Knowledge Divine; who exists even when the intellect does not, as the face exists without a mirror and its reflection.

I am the soul Supreme, the embodied Eternal Self-Gnosis who stands beyond the mind and the senses, who is the Mind of the mind, The Eye of the eye and still imperceptible by any of these.

I am the Soul Supreme, the embodied Self Knowledge Divine who is One and shines on its own; who enlightens varied intellects as the one sun variously reflects in different pots of water.

I am the Soul Supreme, the embodied Self Knowledge Divine who illumines all the intellects at one and the same time, as the sun gives light to all eyes at a time.

I am the Soul Supreme, the embodied Eternal Self Gnosis, whose light gives to the eyes the power of sight like the rising sun allows the vision of the world.

I am the Soul Supreme, the embodied Self Knowledge Divine, The One without a second, who illumines the intellects both firm and unsteady, as the one sun reflects variously in both still and choppy waters.

I am the Soul Supreme, the embodied Self Knowledge Divine, who seems to be bound by a dull intellect, as the sun covered by clouds appears to the foolish lightless and bright.

I am the Soul Supreme, the embodied Eternal Self Gnosis Ever pure, stainless like the ether, the oneself permeating all objects, untouched, untainted by their contact.

Just as the difference between various precious stones arises due to their peculiar color and shape. So, the Supreme Self is felt divided by limiting attributes. As the moon looks to be many and changing in the waters. Oh Vishnu! Thou appearest in varied forms within thy Unity, Purity, and Changelessness.

NIRVANASTAKAM

STANZAS ON LIBERATION.

Adi Shankaracharya

(1) I am neither the conscious nor the subconscious mind. Neither the intellect nor the ego. Neither the ears nor the tongue nor the senses of sight and smell. Neither ether nor air, nor fire, nor water or earth. I am Consciousness and Bliss, I am Shiva, I am shiva.

(2) I am neither the Life force nor the five vital airs.
Neither the seven body components, nor the five Sheaths. Neither speech, nor hands, nor feet nor anus nor the sex organ.
I am consciousness and Bliss, I am Shiva, I am Shiva.

(3) Neither hatred nor attachment, neither avarice, nor infatuation. Neither arrogance, nor jealousy, neither righteous ness, nor wealth, nor pleasure, nor liberation are mine. I am consciousness a Bliss, I am Shiva, I am Shiva.

(4) I am neither virtue nor vice, neither pleasure, nor pain.
Neither Mantra nor sacred place, neither the Vedas, nor sacrifices. I am neither the food nor the eater nor the act of eating. I am Consciousness and Bliss, I am Shiva, I am Shiva.

(5) Neither death nor doubt, nor caste distinction.
Neither father nor Mother, nor even birth are mine, I am neither brother nor friend, neither guru, nor disciple.
I am Consciousness and Bliss, I am Shiva, I am Shiva.

(6) I am mindless, without form. I am all pervasive,
I am everywhere, yet beyond all senses. I am neither detachment nor salvation, nor anything measurable. I am Consciousness and Bliss, I am Shiva, I am Shiva.

GLOSSARY

Abu : Mountain in the north of Gujarat, on the border of Rajasthan.

Adya : Primeval, initial.

Agama: Tantric scripture, in which Lord Shiva is the Guru.

Agni : Fire, Fire Divinity. Ahamkara : Ego sense, egoism, I-am-ness.

Airavata : Mythological elephant with seven tusks, vehicle of Lord Indra, king of celestials.

Ajapa: Automatic repetition of the So Ham Ham Sah mantra, within oneself.

Ajña: Seat of the Guru, the Guru's command,

Ajñana : Ignorance.

Akasha : Ether.

Akshar : Indestructible; letter of the alphabet.

Amrita : Nectar, ambrosia.

Anahata : Unbeaten, natural divine inner sounds.

Ananda : Bliss. Anga : limb. Antar : Inner, within.

Antahkarana : Internal instrument, the Mind in its four aspects.

Anubhuti : Realization.

Anusthan : spiritual process.

Anusvara : Nasal character of the Sanskrit alphabet: represented by a dot, follows a vowel.

Apana : Downward vital air.

Apas : Water.

Aparoksa : Self, direct experience and knowledge.

Asambprajnata : Inhibition of all mental functions, nirvikalpa samadhi.

Asana : Posture, physical exercise.

Ashram : Spiritual community, abode of saints and monks.

Asura : Demon, evil human tendency.

Atharva veda : The fourth of the four Vedas.

Atman: The Self, the inner soul.

Aurobindo : Great Yogi poet and Seer, 20th century.

Avidya : Ignorance, nescience, elusive power.

Avyakta : Unmanifest, undifferentiated, invisible.

Ayurveda : The Veda dealing with medical and herbal science.

Bandha : Yogic seal. Basti : Yogic process of drawing water into the intestines through the anus. .

Bhagavat : Devotional scripture relating the lives of the Avatars of Vishnu.

Bhagavan : The Lord, denomination also given to great saints.

Bhakti : Devotion, divine love.

Bhava : Attitude, purity of thought and feeling.

Bhoga : Enjoyment.

Bija : Seed letter, root.

Bindu : Dot, symbol of divine consciousness.

Bhoot Shuddi : Purificatory process of the three bodies and elements.

Brahma : The creator, first god of the trinity, cosmic intelligence.

Brahman : The absolute reality, Godhead.

Brahmarandra : Aperture of Brahma, fontanelle, top of the skull.

Buddhi : Intellectual faculty, intelligence.

Chakra : Wheel, subtle plexus.

Chandra : The moon.

Chintamani : Mythological stone.

Chit : Consciousness.

Chitta : The subconscious mind, mind stuff.

Chudamani : Crown, shining star.

Darshan : Visit to a saint, divine vision.

Devi : Mother, Goddess.

Dharana : Concentration.

Dharma : Right conduct, duty, morality, religion, enjoined by the scriptures.

Dharma Megha : Cloud of virtue; a particular Samadhi.

Dhatu : Body component, metal.

Dhauti : Yogic process of cleaning the bowels with a longcloth introduced through the mouth.

Dik : Direction.

Diksha : Initiation.

Divya : Divine.

Dhyan : Meditation.

Drik : Seer, perceiver, vision.

Dvapara Yuga : Third era of Hindu mythology.

Ganapati : The elephant faced God, the remover of obstacles.

Gandhi : Mahatma, great karma Yogi, reformer, social worker of India.

Ganesh : Another name for Ganapati, son of Shiva and Parvati.

Ganges : Celestial river, taking its source in the Himalayas flowing into the Bengal gulf.

Gayatri : Form of versification, Goddess Mother of the Vedas.

Girija : Goddess Parvati, wife of Lord Shiva.

Gita : Celestial song; there are 24 Gita's.

Granthi : Knot, made by consciousness at certain levels.

Guna : Quality, attribute, merit. Guru: Spiritual preceptor, master.

Hamsah : Celestial swan, the inner self.

Hanuman : The monkey God, hero of the Ramayana.

Hari : Lord Vishnu, the preserver.

Hatha : The physical aspect of Yoga, meaning the union of the sun and moon.

Hriday : The heart.

Ichcha : Desire, will.

Ida : The duct on the left side of the spine related to the moon.

Indra : The Lord of Celestials.

Indriyas : Sense organ, sense of perception.

Ishtadeveta : The Chosen loved Deity.

Iswara : The Universal being in a causal state.

Jagat : The world, changing.

Jagrat : The waking state.

Jal : Water.

Jalandhar : A yogic seal.

Japa : Repetition of a divine name, mantra.

Jivanmukti : Liberation while yet in the body.

Jivatma : The incarnated soul.

Jnana : Knowledge (spiritual).

Kadamba : A tree (neulia orientalis) fringed ball shaped, prickly flowers.

Kafa : Phlegm, humour of the body.

Kala : Time; quality, Death (Yama).

Kali : The dark Goddess of destruction.

Kali Yuga : The dark age, Iron age.

Kama : Desire.

Kandarpa : A form of vital air.

Kapala : Skull, cranium.

Karan : Cause, reason.

Karma : Action.

Karmic : force of one's accumulated actions.

Kashi : Benares, modern Varanasi.

Kosha : Sheath, scabbard.

Kriya : Yogic process, power of action.

Kubera : The Lord of riches; Mammon.

Kumbhaka : Retention of breath.

Kundalini : The coiled up one, the serpent power.

Lahari : Wave.

Lakshmi : The Goddess of Wealth and prosperity.

Lalita : Melody in India music, name of the Goddess Mother.

Laya : Destruction.

Linga : Symbolic representation of Shiva; gender.

Loka : World, Abode.

Maha : Great.

Mahabharata : Mythological epic relating the war of Kurukshetra.

Mahat : Cosmic intelligence, first product from Nature.

Mahatma : Great Soul, saintly being.

Maheshwar : The Great Lord.

Majja : Body component, marrow.

Makara : A kind of water monster, like a crocodile.

Mala : Rosary, guarland.

Mamsa : Meat.

Manas : Mind, thinking faculty.

Mandala : Mystic diagram, halo, group.

Muni : Gem, diamond.

Mantra : Sacred words or sounds.

Matra : A unit of measurement as in music, prosody.

Matrika : The seed letters of the Sanskrit alphabet, forms of the Mother Goddess.

Maya : The illusive Power, veiling, projecting power of the universe.

Mayic : About Maya.

Meru : Mythological mountain, axis of the universe.

Moda : Delight after acquisition.

Moksha : Liberation, release from the wheel of life and death.

Mukta : Liberated.

Mulbandha : Yogic seal.

Mula : The root.

Mrityunjaya : Vanquisher of death, immortal.

Muni : Hermit, Sage.

Nabhi : Navel.

Nada : Sound.

Nadi : Duct of subtle vital energy.

Nama': name.

Narada : Lord of Sages.

Nauli : Yogic process, curing diseases of the bowels.

Neti : Yogic exercise aiming at the purification of the nostrils.

Nigama : Tantric scripture, in which the Goddess is the Guru.

Nirvana : Liberation, salvation.

Nirvikalpa : superconscious state, Samadhi in which mind has been annihilated.

Nivritti : Renunciation, stepping back from worldly activity.

Niyama : Spiritual rules.

Nyas : Placing of the mantra and deity over the body.

Ojas : Lustre, spiritual power stored up in the brain.

Pada : Foot, one fourth portion.

Padma : Lotus.

Paramananda : Supreme bliss.

Paramahansa : Supreme swan, title given to great saints.

Paramatma : Supreme soul.

Parmeshwara : Supreme lord. Parmeshwari: Supreme goddess.

Paramshiva : Supreme shiva.

Parvati : Consort of Lord Shiva, daughter of Himalaya.

Pashu : Animal, bestial type of man.

Patanjali : Ancient seer, author of the Yoga-sutras, science of Raja Yoga.

Pingala : The duct on the right side of the spine, related to the sun.

Pit : Bile, humour of the body.

Pitha : Abode, seat.

Poorna : Perfect, full, whole, infinite.

Prajapati : Maintainer of subjects, king, Lord Brahma (creator).

Prajna : Intellect, awareness, consciousness, causal state.

Prakasha : Light.

Prakriti : Causal matter, nature.

Pramoda : Pleasure enjoyed with a desired object.

Prana : Vital energy, life force:

Pranava : OM, Udgitha.

Pranayama : Yogic process to control the life force.

Prithvi : Earth.

Pratibha : Genius, talent, supreme light.

Pratista : Prestige, status, installation of power.

Pratyahara : Withdrawing of the senses.

Priya : Joy derived on seeing a beloved object.

Pura : City, complete.

Puranas : Mythological, historical stories of the Hindu scriptures.

Purascharan : A spiritual practice and process.

Purusha : The Supreme Being, the Lord, the Inner Self.

Pushan : Name of the sun, the one nourishing all.

Rajas : Principle of dynamism, generating passion, restlessness, menses.

Raja Yoga : The royal Yoga, Yoga of mental control.

Rakta : Blood.

Rama : The 7th Avatar of Lord Vishnu, incarnation of Purity and righteousness.

Rama Krishna : Great Bengali saint of the end of the 19th century.

Rasa : Essence of enjoyment, juice, sap, sweet feeling.

Rig Veda : Irst of the 4 Vedas.

Rishi : Seer, Sage.

Rudra : Dreadful form of Lord Shiva, great healer.

Rupa : Form, beauty, charm; subtle principle pf color and form.

Rupatita : Beyond form.

SadGuru : Supreme, true and perfect Guru.

Sadhana : Spiritual discipline practice.

SadaShiva : Pure form of Lord Shiva.

Sahaja : Natural state of self-awareness

Sahasrar : The thousand petals lotus.

Sahasranam : The thousand names of God or the Goddess.

Samadhi : The state of super consciousness, meditative absorption of the mind.

Samana : The vital air working digestion."

Samashti : Integrated whole of the same class of entity, macrocosm.

Sama Veda : 3rd of the four Vedas.

Samhara : Annihilation, destruction.

Samhita : Code of conduct found in the Vedas.

Samskaras : Impression, ceremonial purification, prenatal tendency.

Sankalpa : Resolution, determination, desire, imagination.

Sannyasin : Renunciation of social ties, vow of monkhood.

Saraswati : Goddess of Learning, arts; holy river.

Sat : Existence, reality, truth.

Sattva : Principle of purity, reality, clarity, harmony.

Satya : Truth.

Satyavan : Hero of the great poem Savitri composed by Shri Aurobindo.

Satya Yuga : First of the four ages.

Saundarya Lahari : Tantric poem was written on the Great Goddess by Shri Shankaracharya. Wave of beauty.

Savitri : A form of the goddess Gayatri, wife of Brahma (creator).

Shabda : Sound, Vedas, Omkara.

Shakti : Power, divine conscious energy.

Shaktipat : The transference of divine power.

Shakti Chalan : An Hatha yogic process to awake the Kundalini.

Shanti : Peace.

Shankaracharya : Great Siddha Yogi, poet, seer of the 9th century, great reformer of the Hindu religion.

Sharira : Body.

Shiva : The auspicious One, the destroyer form of God.

Shri : Renown, repute, name of the Goddess of wealth and prosperity.

Shuddi : Purification.

Siddha : An accomplished perfect being.

Soma : Moon, celestial beverage, ambrosia, elixir.

Spanda : Pulsation, throbbing.

Sparsha : Touch, sense of touch (subtle element)

Sristi : Creation.

Sthiti : Maintenance.

Stotra : Hymn, eulogy of a god.

Sthula : Physical.

Sukra : Planet Venus, semen, Friday.

Sukshma : Subtle, fine, invisible.

Sumeru : Mythological mountain of gold.

Surya : The sun.

Sushumna : The central duct in the spine.

Sushupti : Deep sleep state without dreams.

Sutra : Form of versification utilized in certain scriptures.

Svapna : Dream, illusion.

Svastika : Auspicious sign, cross, symbol of the rotation of the Universe.

Svayambhu : Self born.

Swami : Name to renunciates and great saints.

Taijasa : Vedantic term to designate an individual in the subtle state.

Tamas : Ignorance, inertia, darkness.

Tandra : A special meditative state, like a trance.

Tanmatra : Atom, rudimentary element.

Tantra : The most recent Hindu esoteric scriptures.

Tantric : Belonging to the Tantras.

Tatparya : Purport, substance.

Tattva : Principle, reality, essence, element.

Tejas : Brilliance, lustre, heat, the fire element.

Tratak : A form of concentration of eye on some object.

Treta Yuga : The third age.

Trikona : Triangle: symbol of Shakti.

Trikuti : Third eye

Tripura : Name of the goddess.

Tulsidas : Great poet saint of the north of India, 16th century; author of the 'Ramacharitmanas' a Ramayana in Hindi.

Turya : Superconscious state, pure self-awareness.

Udana : The vital air with an upward flow.

Uddiyanbandha : A yogic seal.

Unmani :A yogic state, mindless state.

Upanishad : Hindu scriptures, latter art of the Vedas.

Upasak : Devout spiritual practitioner.

Upaprana : Subsidiary vital airs.

Urdhvareta : Perfect celibate, whose seminal fluid flows to the brain.

Vahni : Fire.

Vaishnava : Belonging to the cult of Vishnu and his avatars (emanations)

Varshini : The goddess showering.

Varuna : Lord of waters and the ocean.

Vasanas : Subtle desire, subtle impression.

Vasishtha : Great seer, born of Brahma's mind; guru of : Lord Rama.

Vat : Wind, humor.

Vayu : Wind (vital air). The Wind God.

Vedanta : End of the Vedas, the Upanishads.

Vedas : Highest authority among the Aryans of India, most ancient scripture, divinely created.

Vidhan : Piercing, opening of the chakras.

Vedic : Belonging to the Vedas.

Vidya : Knowledge, learning, esoteric science.

Vira : Warrior, active type of man. Viraj : Seated (honour).

Vishnu : The second in the trinity, the maintainer.

Visva : Cosmos, a name of the Jiva in the waking state.

Viveka: Discrimination, between the real and the world.

Vivekananda : The leading disciple of Shri Ram Krishna, first expounder of Hinduism in the West.

Vritti: Thought wave, mental modification.

Vyana : The vital air pervading the whole body.

Vyashti : Individual.

Yajur Veda : The third of the four Vedas.

Yama : God of Death, mental discipline.

Yantra : Mystic diagram.

Yoga : Union with the Supreme Godhead.

Yogic : Pertaining to Yoga.

Yogi : Practising Yoga.

Yoni : Female Organ, triangle symbol of Shakti.

Yukta : Combined, joined.

BIBLIOGRAPHY

The Synthesis of Yoga: **Shri Aurobindo.**

The Riddle of the World: **Shri Aurobindo.**

Lights on Yoga : **Shri Aurobindo.**

Bases of Yoga : **Shri Aurobindo.**

More Lights on Yoga : **Shri Aurobindo.**

Devatma Shakti : **Swami Vishnu tirth.**

Shakti Hidden Treasure of Power: **Shri Dhyan Yogi Madhusudandas.**

Light on Meditation : **Shri Dhyan Yogi Madhusudandas.**

Message to Disciples: **Shri Dhyan Yogi Madhusudandas.**

Chiti Shakti Vilas : **Swami Muktananda.**

Kundalini the Secret of Life : **Swami Muktananda.**

Raja Yoga : **Swami Vivekananda.**

Kundalini Yoga : **Swami Shivananda.**